CHICKEN
AND POULTRY COOKBOOK

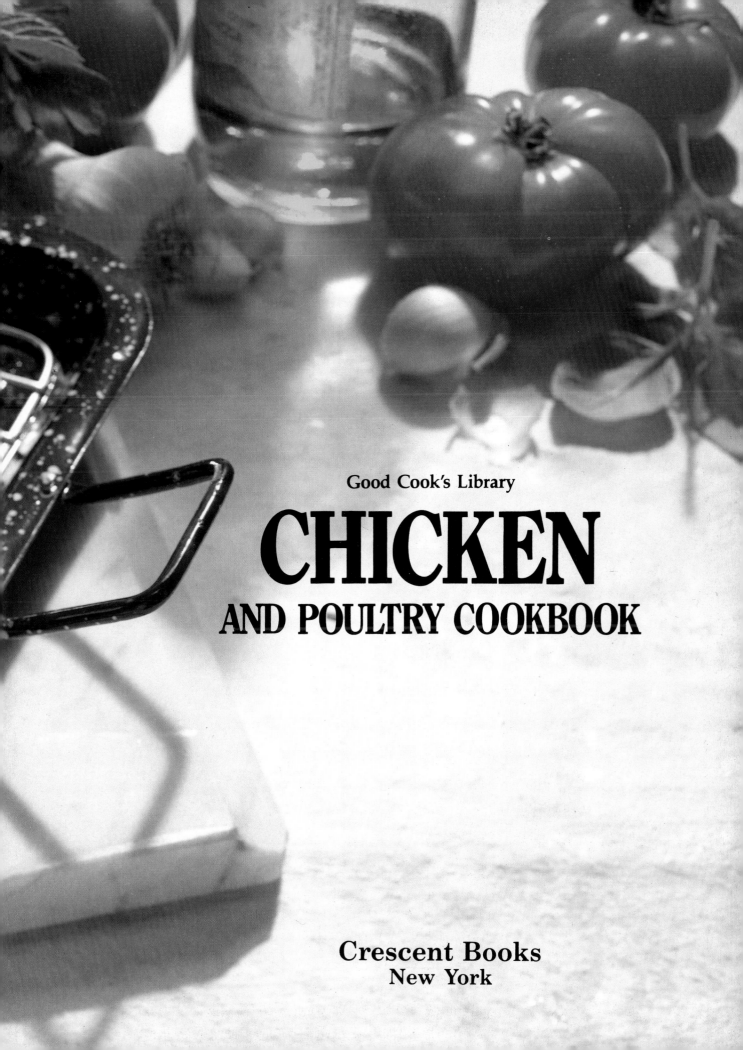

Good Cook's Library

CHICKEN
AND POULTRY COOKBOOK

Crescent Books
New York

ISBN 0-517-66211-6
h g f e d c b a

Contents

Tips for Cooking Poultry

Drawing Poultry

A bird that is not oven ready has to be drawn.

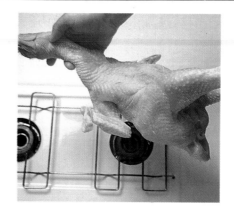

If there are any small feathers left after plucking, hold the bird over an open flame (gas burner, lighted taper, piece of burning paper) turning it quickly.

Chicken Pieces

For many casseroles pieces are required. A small chicken cuts into 4 pieces, a heavier bird into 6, and a duck, goose, or turkey into 8–12 pieces.

Cut the thigh at the joint, likewise with the wings.

Boning out chicken breast

Start boning at the neck.

Cut the skin at the neck, peel it back.

Stuffing Poultry

Never fill the neck or the stomach of a bird too full.

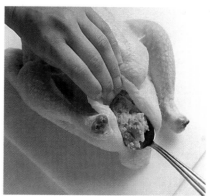

When filling the tailend leave a space for closing the bird.

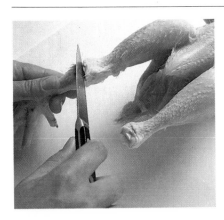

Cut head and neck off, pull out the gullet, windpipe, and gizzard. Cut off the feet at the first joint of the leg.

Cut across the rump, and remove the entrails. Rub one tablespoon salt inside the carcass and wash out with water.

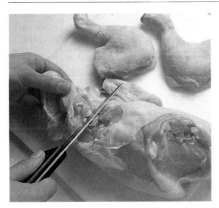

In a big bird the thigh is cut twice.

Ease the torso in half, having cut through it lengthways with poultry scissors. The back and small discarded pieces can be used for soup or sauce.

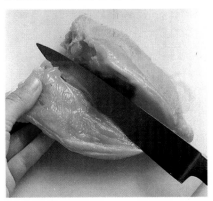

Cut through the breastbone lengthways.

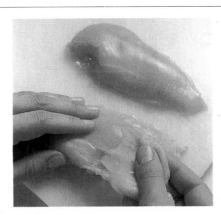

Ease the flesh off the bone.

Cut into pieces, and gently remove any skin by hand.

Both openings should be sewn together with a thick darning needle, and kitchen string. Close the opening from the back down, and sew across.

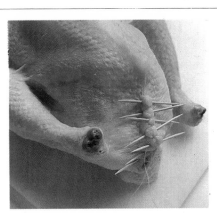

The opening can also be closed with small wooden skewers, to keep the stuffing in.

Tips for Cooking Poultry

Trussing

The object of trussing is to keep the bird in good shape, making it easy to carve.

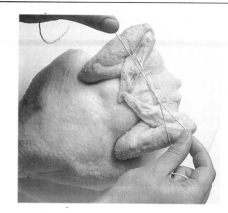

Fold the wings back neatly over the back of the carcass. Use a large needle and string, pushed through the carcass, and tied over the folded back wings.

To Prevent Burning

Young poultry, without much fat, will burn easily during cooking.

Before trussing place slices of fresh bacon over the breast, and tie in place securely.

Cooking on a Spit

Poultry cooked on a spit must be neatly trussed to turn easily.

A large chicken can hinder the shaft rotating on a rotisserie.

To Casserole Poultry

The bird must be covered in salted water, on a low heat. Add spices to the trussed bird, and leave it to simmer for 1 ½ hours.

Add vegetables, cloves, bay leaves, onion and soup greens about 30 minutes before the end of cooking time.

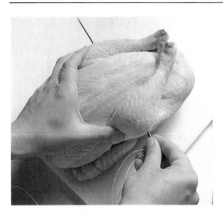

Likewise insert a large needle and string through the middle of the bird and tie at the top keeping the legs in place.

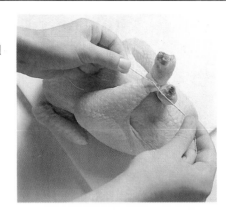

Or, tie the two legs together over the breast.

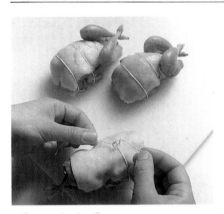

Very small birds need to have a large piece of bacon fat tied securely over the complete breast and top.

For festive occasions weave 1 inch wide piece of bacon like a mat over the bird and fix securely in place.

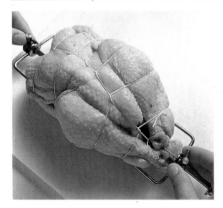

Size is not important when cooking over wood or coal.

Securely fix the bird to the spit with holding forks to prevent it from roasting unevenly through rotating improperly.

During cooking, skim off any froth from the top of water.

Allow 2 medium sized carrots per person and 2 well washed leeks tied up in a bundle per person.

Stuffings

Apple and Chestnut Stuffing

This stuffing is for many families the traditional "Christmas Stuffing" for turkey and goose. It also goes very well with duck and wild duck. Chestnuts can be substituted with pitted prunes soaked in a little dry white wine. To stretch the filling for bigger birds use toasted white bread cubes and chopped almonds. For game birds the apples can be replaced by halved seedless grapes. The following quantities are enough for a medium-sized bird:

Peel, core and cut 2 cups cooking apples into 8 wedges and marinate in dry red wine until the apples look slightly pink. This takes approximately 2 hours.

Ground Meat Stuffing

This stuffing goes well with most poultry. It is especially useful for increasing serving capacity. Particularly for fatty animals, lamb or lean ground beef stuffing is suitable; whereas for lean animals mixed ground meat or pork can be used. To make this stuffing lighter use soaked bread rolls or breadcrumbs and eggs, mixed with the chopped giblets and herbs. Our recipe:

Soak 1 or 2 stale bread rolls in cold water. Dice 3 shallots and fry until golden brown. Squeeze dry the bread rolls and mix with ¾-1 lb ground meat, 2 eggs, shallots, ½ teaspoon salt, pinch of dried sage, pinch of ground coriander. Mix to a moist but firm consistency.

Bread Stuffing

This stuffing is usually recommended when poultry is being eaten with only vegetables or a salad. While this stuffing might not be considered very interesting, however it can be piquantly seasoned and combined with unusual ingredients. Suggestions for stuffing mixtures are: dried fruit soaked in wine, freshly chopped herbs, roasted and chopped almonds, raisins and sultanas, pickled ginger root, roasted sesame or sunflower seeds, diced ham or chopped giblets slightly fried giblets. Our recipe:

According to the size of the bird, grate 3 or 4 stale bread rolls with a square grater. Cut the bread rolls in half and soak in a light white wine.

Buckwheat Stuffing

This stuffing makes a very nutritious and substantial meal, with no need for rich accompaniments. Season the filling to taste and add ingredients with distinct flavors. Mushrooms, garlic, gomasio (sesame-sea salt mixture), freshly chopped herbs, sweetcorn, spinach, celery, and onions are particularly good. You can also use rice (brown rice, wild rice) green rye, millet or par-boiled red lentils instead of the buckwheat for this stuffing. Our recipe:

Roast approximately 4 cups roughly ground buckwheat in a dry frying pan until golden brown, stirring constantly. Allow to cool.

Nick 2 cups chestnuts with a sharp knife and bake them in a medium oven for 30 minutes until their skins crack. After 10 minutes pour 1 cup of cold water on the baking sheet, to avoid the chestnuts drying out. Peel the slightly cooled chestnuts and mix with the drained apples.

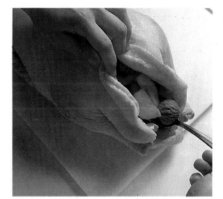

Mix ½ cup of oil with a pinch of white pepper and paprika; then rub the bird inside and out. Rub the inside with ½ tea-spoon salt. Stuff the bird with the apple and chestnut filling. Sew up the openings with thread and frequently baste the bird during cooking with the seasoned oil. Finally brush the bird with red wine.

Take the meat from the gizzard, remove the thick gray skin, then dice to-gether with the heart and liver. Fry in bubbling but-ter for 3 minutes, stirring constantly. Then mix with 2 tablespoons of chopped chives an the ground meat.

Rub the poultry with a mixture of a pinch of salt, dried sage and ground coriander. Then stuff the bird with the ground meat stuffing, sew up the open-ings, truss and roast the bird until crisp and golden brown.

Fry 4-6 oz diced ham in bubbling butter for 3 min-utes, stirring constantly, together with sliced mush-rooms and diced giblets.

Squeeze dry the bread rolls and mix with salt, pepper, 1 teaspoon chopped ginger, 2 tablespoons soya sauce and 2 tablespoons chopped and roasted almonds and 1-2 eggs. Combine with the mushroom mixture and stuff the bird. Before com-pletion of cooking (about 15-30 minutes before), brush the bird with the white wine left from soak-ing the bread rolls.

Clean 2 celery sticks, 2 medium onions and 2 garlic cloves, chop and fry in butter until the onions are transparent. Add the buckwheat and 1 cup white wine, cover and slightly simmer for 5 min-utes.

Mix the stuffing with 1 teaspoon freshly chopped thyme, 1 tablespoon - sesame oil and enough buckwheat to bind the stuffing. Season the mix-ture with salt, add dried thyme and fold in 2 stiffly beaten egg whites.

Recommended Cooking Times

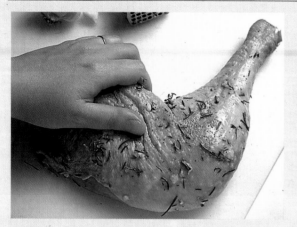

1) Before cooking, rub any spices into the washed and well-dried flesh, to penetrate the skin.

2) During roasting of large fatty birds, pierce the skin with a thin wooden skewer to release the fat.

3) Small birds (or portions) cooked in a marinade need to be basted often during roasting to prevent them drying out.

	Boil	Casserole	Braise	Fry
Chicken 100 oz-1 lb 2 oz		50 minutes	25-30 minutes	350°F 5 minutes 310°F 25 minutes (1 bird)
Fat Chicken	1 ¼-2 lbs	1 ½ hours	35-40 minutes	350°F 6 minutes 310°F 25 minutes (half bird)
Roasting Chicken	2 ¼ lbs-3 ¼ lbs	1 ½ hours	35-45 minutes	350°F 8 minutes 310°F 30 minutes (½ bird)
Fat Chicken 2 ¾ lbs-3 ½ lbs	1-1 ¾ hours	1 ½-2 hours	45 minutes	350°F 10 minutes
Capon	3 ¼ lbs-4 ½ lbs	3 hours	1 hour	
Broiling fowl for Soup 3 ¾ lbs-4 ½ lbs	2 hours			
Guinea Fowl 2 lbs-2 ¾ lbs	1 hour	1 ½ hours	35-45 minutes	350°F 6 minutes
Pigeon 10 oz-¾ lb	1 hour		30-50 minutes	310°F 25 minutes (1 bird)
Young Duck	3 ½ lbs-4 lbs		50-70 minutes	
Duck 5 lbs-11 lbs			60-80 minutes	
Goose 11 lbs-13 ¼ lbs			1 ½-2 hours	
Turkey 4 ½ lbs-6 ¾ lbs				
Turkey 11 lbs				
Pheasant 2 ¼ lbs	1 hour		40-60 minutes	
Partridge ¼ lbs-14 oz			20-50 minutes	
Quail ¼ lb-7 oz		30-40 minutes	25-40 minutes	
Wild Duck 2 ¼ lbs-4 ½ lbs	2 hours		1-1 ½ hours	
Young Goose 9 lbs			1 ¼—1 ½ hours	

A cooking chart is not foolproof. Cooking and roasting times are dependent on the age and quality of the bird and how long the oven will keep an even heat. Therefore it is essential to check from time to time how the bird is cooking and to lower or raise the heat accordingly.

	Roast	Electric
Chicken 10 oz-1 lb 2 oz	Stuffed	425°F 20 minutes 30 minutes
Fat Chicken 1 ¼ lbs-2 lbs	Stuffed	425°F 35-40 minutes 40-45 minutes
Roasting Chicken 2 ¼ lbs-3 ¼ lbs	Stuffed	425°F 40-60 minutes 50-60 minutes
Fat Chicken 2 ¾ lbs	Stuffed	425°F 1 hour 1 ¼-1 ½ hours
Capon 3 ¼ lbs-4 ½ lbs	Stuffed	425°F 1-1 ¼ hours 1 ½-1 ½ hours
Hen for soup 3 ¾ lbs-4 ½ lbs		
Guinea Fowl 2 lbs-2 ¾ lbs	Stuffed	400°F 30-45 minutes 45-60 minutes
Pigeon 300-400 g 10 oz-¾ lb	Stuffed	425°F 20-30 minutes 30-45 minutes
Young Duck	Stuffed	425°F 1-1 ½ hours 1 ¼-1 ¾ hours
Duck 5 lbs-11 lbs	Stuffed	350°F 2 hours 2 ½ hours
Young Goose 9 lbs	Stuffed	350°F 2 ½ hours 3 hours
Goose 11 lbs-13 ¼ lbs	Stuffed	335°F 3 ½ hours 4 hours
Young Turkey 4 ½ lbs-6 ¾ lbs	Stuffed	350°F 2 ½ hours 3 hours
Turkey Hen 11 lbs	Stuffed	335°F 3 hours 3 ½ hours
Pheasant 2 ¼ lbs	Stuffed	425°F 30-40 minutes 45-60 minutes
Partridge ¼ lbs-14 oz	Stuffed	425°F 35-40 minutes 45-50 minutes
Quail ¼ lb-7 oz	Stuffed	425°F 20 minutes 30 minutes
Wild Duck 2 ¼ lbs-4 ½ lbs	Stuffed	350°F 1 ½ hours 1 ¾-2 hours

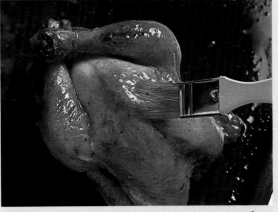

4) To make a crispy finish, brush the skin with marinade, salt, honey and water, beer or wine about 15-30 minutes before a large bird has finished roasting.

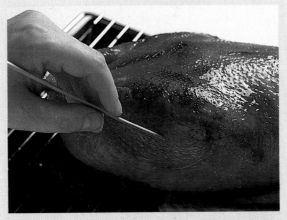

5) To prevent overcooking, pierce the skin from time to time until the juices are no longer a red or rosy color (two-thirds of the way through cooking.

6) Cover the bird loosely with aluminum foil and put under the oven grill (10 minutes before carving).

Soups
and
Stews

Chicken Consommé

Economical and widely appreciated

400 calories per serving
Thawing time: 4 hours
Preparation time: 10 minutes
Cooking time: 2 hours

2¼ lbs. frozen chicken giblets
2 qts. water
2 tsp. salt
1 leek
2 carrots
2 sprigs celery tops
2 sprigs parsley
1 onion
½ bay leaf
1 clove
4 white peppercorns
4 egg yolks
2 tbs. chopped chives

R emove giblets from wrapping and allow to thaw in a sieve placed over a bowl. Pour away any water that collects during the process. • Wash the giblets, put into a large saucepan with the water, salt and bring to a boil. Turn down the heat so that the bouillion barely simmers. Skim off any scum that forms during the first 30 minutes. Simmer gently for another hour, until the bouillion is reduced by half. • Meanwhile, wash the leak, removing the green part, and cut lengthwise into strips. Peel and wash the carrots and cut in rounds. Wash the celery tops, herbs, peel the onion and spike the bay leaf into it with the clove. • Add prepared vegetables and peppercorns to bouillon after it has simmered for the first hour and a half, cover the pan and simmer 30 minutes longer. • Put one egg yolk into each of 4 soup bowls. Pour the bouillion into a separate bowl through a fine sieve or a piece of muslin. If you wish to remove all fat from the stock it must be left to cool, then the solidified fat can be removed and the consommé reheated. Pour the consommé over the egg yolks in the soup bowls and serve sprinkled with chives.

Tip: The leek and carrot may be finely chopped and served in the consommé.

Chicken Consomme with Tiny Dumplings

Quick and simple to make

380 calories per serving
Preparation and cooking time: 30 minutes

1 lb. chicken breast
2 shallots
1 tsp. salt
Pinch white pepper
Pinch dried thyme
⅔ cup fine breadcrumbs
1 tbs. chopped parsley
1 egg
¼ cup cream
4 cups chicken bouillon
1¼ cups frozen peas

G rind the meat, either in a meat grinder or a food-processor. • Peel shallots and chop very finely before mixing them with the ground chicken, salt, pepper, thyme, breadcrumbs, parsley and egg, with sufficient cream to give a mixture that is not too stiff. • Bring the bouillon to a boil with the peas, reduce heat to simmer gently. • Shape the chicken mixture into little dumplings, using 2 teaspoons dipped in cold water. Put dumplings into simmering bouillon and cook gently for 10 minutes. • Serve soup immediately.

Cream of Chicken Soup

Classic recipe requiring a certain amount of time

930 calories per serving
Preparation time: 40 minutes
Cooking time: 2 hours

1 stewing chicken weighing 2¼ lbs.	
2 qts. water	
2 tsp. salt	
3 leeks	
1 large carrot	
1 stick celery	
1 onion	
½ bay leaf	
2 cloves	
4 white peppercorns	
2 tbs. butter	
3 tbs. flour	
2 egg yolks	
½ cup cream	

Wash chicken thoroughly inside and out, bring to a boil with water and salt, reduce heat until water simmers very gently. Skim off any scum that forms during the first 30 minutes. • Simmer for 2 hours altogether, until broth is reduced by a good half. • Remove green leaves from leeks, wash white part thoroughly. Peel, wash and slice carrot. Rinse celery and slice. Peel onion and spike bay leaf onto it with cloves. • After broth has simmered for 1½ hours, add prepared vegetables and peppercorns and simmer, covered, for remaining 30 minutes. • Lift chicken out of broth, remove breast fillets and slice. • Strain broth, allow to cool and remove fat. Slice leeks. Melt butter, sauté flour in it, gradually add 1½ qts. broth and simmer gently for 10 minutes. • Add sliced chicken breast and leek to soup. • Beat egg yolks and cream together and use to thicken soup.

Delicate Chicken Soup

Hungarian specialty

480 calories per serving
Preparation time: 30 minutes
Cooking time: 1½ hours

1 chicken weighing 2¼ lbs.
6 cups water
Bunch flat-leaved parsley
1 tsp. salt
2 cups cooking apples
1 tsp. honey
1 tbs. oatmeal
½ cup sour cream
1 egg yolk

Wash the chicken, cut into 8 pieces and bring to a boil in the water. Reduce heat so that it barely simmers, continually skimming off any scum that forms during the first 30 minutes. • Rinse and shake dry the parsley, then chop the leaves and put to one side, covered. • Add the parsley stalks with the salt to the broth and simmer for 50 minutes longer. • Peel and quarter the apples, remove core and cut into thin slices before cooking gently in a covered saucepan with ¼ cup water and the honey until they are just soft. • Remove parsley stalks and chicken pieces from broth, separate the meat from the skin and bones and dice it. • Toast the oatmeal to a light brown, stir into the sour cream and add to the soup. Simmer for 5 minutes more. • Add the cubed chicken and apple slices to the soup and reheat, then remove from the heat. • Beat the egg yolk with 2 tbs. of the hot soup and use this mixture to thicken the soup, before sprinkling with the chopped parsley.

Spicy Chicken Soup

Simple but delicious

260 calories per serving
Thawing time: 4 hours
Preparation time: 20 minutes
Cooking time: 1 hour

1 lb. frozen chicken giblets
6 cups water
1 tsp. salt
1 pkg. frozen soup vegetables
1 onion
½ lb. chicken breast, boned
½ cup button mushrooms
1 tbs. butter
1 tbs. curry powder
Pinch cayenne pepper
Chives

Place the unwrapped chicken giblets in a sieve over a bowl to thaw, throwing away any water that collects in the process. • Wash the giblets thoroughly, place in a saucepan, cover with the water and bring to a boil. Remove any scum as it forms. • After 30 minutes cooking time, add salt and soup vegetables and continue to simmer gently for another 30 minutes. • Meanwhile, peel and chop finely onion, cut chicken breasts into thin strips, clean and slice mushrooms. • Heat butter in heavy pan and fry chopped onion gently with chicken strips, turning frequently, until both are done. Add sliced mushrooms and fry 1 minute longer, then stir in curry powder and cayenne pepper. • Strain chicken broth over chicken strips and vegetables and keep hot. Discard giblets. • Rinse chives before chopping finely and sprinkling over soup.

Cream of Chicken Soup with Banana

Economical and easy to prepare

380 calories per serving
Thawing time: 4 hours
Preparation time: 440 minutes
Cooking time: 1 hour, 10 minutes

1 lb. frozen chicken giblets	
5 cups water	
1 tsp. salt	
1 pkg. frozen soup vegetables	
1 small onion	
¼ cup butter	
2 tbs. flour	
1 cooking apple	
2 bananas	
¼ cup cream	
2 tsp. lemon juice	
Pinch white pepper	
1 tbs. flaked almonds	

Unwrap giblets and allow to thaw, then wash them and bring to a boil in the water. Skim off scum as it forms. After about 30 minutes add the salt and soup vegetables. Continue to simmer 30 minutes longer. • Strain the broth and take any meat off the bone. • Peel and chop onion, then fry in butter until transparent. Sprinkle with flour, continue to fry a little longer, then stir in broth gradually. Add meat. Simmer gently for 10 minutes longer. • Peel and finely grate the apple. Peel the bananas, mash one of them and mix into the soup together with the cream and grated apple. • Season to taste with lemon juice and pepper, serve garnished with sliced banana and toasted almond flakes.

Cream of Chicken Soup with Asparagus

Wholefood recipe

490 calories per serving
Preparation time: 30 minutes
Cooking time: 1¾ hours

Soup vegetables (e.g. onion, leek, carrot, small piece of celery or celery root, turnip)	
½ small stewing chicken weighing 1¾ lbs.	
7 cups water	
1 bay leaf	
5 white peppercorns	
1 tsp. sea salt	
1¾ cups fresh asparagus	
¾ cups green peas, shelled	
½ cup graham flour	
1 cup cream	
2 egg yolks	
Pinch seasoning salt	
Juice of ½ lemon	
2 tbs. freshly chopped chervil	

Prepare, wash and chop the soup vegetables in small pieces. • Wash the chicken, cover with the water and bring to a boil together with the soup vegetables, bay leaf and peppercorns. Add the salt. Simmer 1½ hours. • Wash the asparagus and peel the woody end thinly. Cut off the tips about 2 in. down and put aside. • Cut the remaining asparagus stalks into small pieces and add to the broth for the final 10 minutes of the cooking time. Strain the broth and measure out 4 cups of it. Bring this to a boil again before adding the cooked asparagus pieces, asparagus tips and peas. Simmer 5 minutes more. • Take chicken meat off the bone, chop in pieces and add to the soup. • Mix the flour to a paste with 1 cup cold broth, pour into soup, simmer gently for 5 minutes, stirring constantly, then remove from heat. • Beat the cream with egg yolks and

use to thicken the soup. Season to taste with seasoning salt and lemon juice, sprinkle with chopped chervil.

Turkey and Vegetable Soup

Requires a certain amount of time

330 calories per serving
Preparation time: 15 minutes
Cooking time: 1¼ hours

1¾ lb. turkey meat
2 tbs. oil
2 qts. hot water
1 tsp. salt
1 onion
Soup vegetables (see index)
2 carrots
1 kohlrabi or white turnip
¾ cup each green beans, shelled peas and cauliflower florets

Pinch white pepper
1 tsp. soy sauce
Handful chervil

Rinse and dry meat. Heat oil in a saucepan, add meat and brown thoroughly, add the water and salt and bring to a boil. • Peel onion, prepare and rinse soup vegetables, add all to soup. Simmer for 1 hour. During first 30 minutes, remove any scum that forms, then cover pan with lid, but allowing some steam to escape. • Peel and wash carrots, slice in thin rounds. Peel and dice kohlrabi or turnip, wash beans and cut in pieces. • Take meat, onion and soup vegetables out of broth by pouring broth through a sieve. Return broth to pan, add carrots, kohlrabi, beans, peas and cauliflower, and simmer for 15 minutes. • Dice meat. Wash and chop chervil. • Return meat to soup, heat

through, season with salt, pepper and soy sauce and sprinkle with chopped chervil.

Pigeon Cream Soup

Requires a certain amount of time

430 calories per serving
Preparation time: 40 minutes
Cooking time: 1 hour

2 prepared pigeons weighing 14 oz. each
6 cups water
1 tsp. salt
Strip lemon peel
1 small onion
2 leeks
Small piece celery root
Sprig each parsley, thyme and dill
2 egg yolks
5 tbs. heavy cream

1 tbs. fresh dill tips

Wash birds well inside and out, put into a large pan with the water, salt and lemon peel and simmer gently for 30 minutes. Skim off scum continuously as it forms. • Wash and dry unpeeled onion, halve it and put cut sides down on a burner to brown. • Take the white part of leeks only, wash and cut into fine strips. Peel, rinse and dice celery root. Rinse herbs and tie together. • Add prepared vegetables and herbs to broth and continue to simmer, half-covered, for 30 minutes. By the end of this time the liquid should be reduced by half. • Strain the soup. Remove the skin and bones from the pigeons and dice the meat before returning it to the soup. Beat egg yolks with heavy cream, combine with 3 tbs. hot broth and stir into soup. • Serve the soup sprinkled with dill tips.

Duck Soup in a Pastry Bonnet

Slightly more complicated

550 calories per serving
Preparation time: 40 minutes
Baking time: 10 minutes

1¼ cups frozen puff pastry sheets
9 oz. duck breast
1 tsp. oil
Pinch each, salt and freshly ground white pepper
2 scallions
1¼ cup zucchini
½ cup button mushrooms
3 cups strong chicken bouillon
6 oz. mildly flavored sausage meat
Bunch chervil
¼ cup cream
1 egg yolk

Allow 4 sheets of puff pastry to thaw, returning the rest of the package to the freezer. • Wash and dry duck breast before browning first the skin side in oil, then turning and completing the process in 3 minutes. Season with salt and pepper. • Clean and wash scallions, then chop in rings. Wash, dry and dice zucchini finely. Clean and rinse mushrooms, then slice them. • Heat the chicken bouillon. • Put sausage meat into a bowl, add to it the washed and finely chopped chervil, 2 tbs. cream and some pepper. Mix well before shaping teaspoonfuls into little dumplings and simmering them gently in the bouillon for 10 minutes. • Cut the duck into fine strips and divide it together with the finely chopped vegetables between four soup bowls. • Preheat oven to 425°F. • Roll pastry out to form circles ¾ in. bigger than the diameter of the bowls. Beat egg yolk with remaining cream. • Fill bowls with hot soup and dumplings. Cover with a pastry lid and glaze with egg yolk. • Bake in center of oven for about 10 minutes until pastry is well browned.

Ujhazy Chicken Soup

Hungarian specialty

600 calories per serving
Preparation time: 30 minutes
Cooking time: 1¼ hours

½ stewing chicken weighing 1½ lbs.
½ cup celery root
½ cup carrot
½ cup cauliflower
1 large onion
1 clove garlic
1½ tsp. salt
6 black peppercorns
1 beefsteak tomato
½ cup shelled peas
½ cup vermicelli

Wash stewing chicken thoroughly. Peel celery root and carrots, then rinse and halve them before cutting one half of each into julienne strips. • Rinse cauliflower and break into florets. • Peel onion and garlic. • Cover chicken with cold water and bring to a boil, skimming off scum as it forms. • Add salt, peppercorns, whole pieces of celery root and carrot, onion, garlic and quartered tomato to chicken and boil for 1 hour. • Boil peas, cauliflower florets and julienne strips, covered, in small amount of water for 10 minutes, then strain. • Cook vermicelli for 3 minutes in 2 cups boiling water and drain. • Remove chicken from stock, separate chicken meat from skin and bones, dice into small pieces and put with vermicelli and vegetables into a tureen. • Strain the soup over this mixture and serve.

Squire's Pheasant Soup

Polish specialty

550 calories per serving
Preparation time: 45 minutes
Cooking time: 1½ hours

1 pheasant weighing 2¼ lbs.
1½ tsp. salt
6 black peppercorns
1 bay leaf
6 cups water
1 celery root
2 carrots
1 small leek
3 tbs. sunflower oil
1 tbs. graham flour
½ cup cream
Bunch parsley

Rinse pheasant, bring to a boil together with salt, peppercorns, bay leaf and water, repeatedly skimming off scum as it forms. • Continue to cook, uncovered, over a gentle heat for 1 hour. • Remove cooked pheasant from broth. Strain broth. • Peel celery root, peel carrots, and slice thinly. Clean and rinse leek and cut in thin rounds. • Heat oil and brown prepared vegetables in it. • Sprinkle with flour, fry for a little while longer, then gradually stir in broth. Simmer soup for 10 minutes. • Discard skin and bones of pheasant and chop the meat. • Return meat to broth and reheat, then stir in cream. • Rinse and dry parsley thoroughly, then chop finely. • Serve soup sprinkled with chopped parsley.

Sapporo Chicken Soup

Japanese specialty, rather expensive

260 calories per serving
Preparation time: 45 minutes
Cooking time: 15 minutes

1 lb. 2 oz. boned chicken breast
1 small white radish
1 small carrot
1 cup potatoes
1 leek, white part only (about 2 oz.)
1 cup green beans
2 tbs. coconut oil
4 cups rich chicken bouillon
5 tbs. soy sauce
2 tsp. honey
1–2 pinches salt
1 tsp. green peppercorns
¼ lb. shrimp

Rinse, pat dry and cube chicken pieces. • Peel and rinse radish, then cut into strips the size of matchsticks. Peel carrot and potatoes, rinse and dry, cut into similar strips. Repeat process with leak, and green beans. • Heat coconut oil. Fry cubes of chicken in it, add vegetables and continue to fry for a few minutes, constantly turning. • Heat chicken bouillon and pour onto vegetables. Cover pan and simmer for 15 minutes, then season with soy sauce, honey, salt and green peppercorns. Finally add shrimp and reheat gently.

Guinea Fowl with Zucchini

Classic recipe, quick and easy

310 calories per serving
Preparation time: 30 minutes
Cooking time: 1 hour

1 guinea fowl weighing 1¾ lb.
1 tsp. salt
6 cups water
1 onion
½ bay leaf
1 clove
2¼ cups zucchini
1 bunch watercress

Wash guinea fowl thoroughly, inside and outside, put in pan with salt and water and bring to a boil. • Peel onion and use the clove to spike the bay leaf into it. • During the first 30 minutes of the cooking time, skim off any scum that forms. At the end of this time, add onion and simmer 20 minutes longer, until a scant half of the liquid has evaporated. • Rinse, dry and cube zucchini. Rinse and dry watercress thoroughly, remove any thick stalks and cut leaves into thin strips. • Add diced zucchini to the broth and cook for 10 minutes. • Lift guinea fowl and onion from broth. Allow broth to simmer, covered while preparing meat. • Take meat from bones, cut in pieces and return to soup. • Serve sprinkled with watercress.

Mulligatawny

Economical specialty

450 calories per serving
Preparation time: 35 minutes
Cooking time: 45 minutes

1 cup long grain rice
5 cups chicken bouillon
1 lb. 2 oz. skinned chicken breast, boned
1 carrot
1 leek, white part only (½ cup)
2 tbs. coconut oil
¼ cup white raisins
1 cooking apple
1 tbs. curry powder
Good pinch cayenne pepper
¼ cup desiccated coconut

Rinse rice in colander under running water until water runs clear. • Bring chicken bouillon to a boil, pour in rice and boil moderately fast, uncovered, for 20 minutes. • Cut chicken in small cubes. Peel carrot in warm water, dry and dice. Wash leek thoroughly in warm water and slice in rounds. • Heat coconut oil in a large pan. First fry chicken cubes until nicely browned, then remove from pan and fry prepared vegetables in remaining oil. Add chicken and vegetables, with as little oil as possible, to rice and broth. • Cover white raisins with hot water, changing water as necessary, until nice and plump. Strain. Rinse, dry, peel and grate apple, then add to soup with white raisins. • Season soup to taste with curry powder and cayenne pepper and sprinkle with coconut before serving.

Chicken and Rice Stew

Economical and simple to prepare

640 calories per serving
Preparation time: 30 minutes
Cooking time: 1 hour and 20 minutes

6 cups water
1 chicken weighing 2¼ lbs.
Sprig each, tarragon, parsley, celery leaves and thyme
1 leek, white part only, (½ cup)
2 shallots
1 tsp. salt
2¼ cups peas
1 cup carrots
1 cup long grain rice
Pinch cayenne pepper
2 tbs. chopped parsley

Bring water to a boil and cook rinsed chicken in it for 30 minutes, skimming off scum as it forms. • Rinse herbs and tie together, wash leek and slice in rounds. Peel and quarter shallots. • When chicken has boiled for 30 minutes, add herbs, leek, shallots and salt to pan, cover and cook for another 30 minutes. • Shell peas. Peel, rinse and dice carrots. Put rice in a sieve and wash under cold running water until water runs clear. Drain. • Take chicken and herbs out of broth. Add vegetables and rice to broth, cover and simmer on low heat for 20 minutes. • Remove chicken meat from carcass and cut in small pieces, then return to pot. Season to taste with cayenne pepper and serve sprinkled with chopped parsley.

Chicken and Vegetable Stew

Simple to prepare and economical

520 calories per serving
Preparation and cooking time: 1¼ hours

1 chicken weighing 2¼ lbs.
1 onion
1 carrot (½ cup)
2 leeks (1 cup)
3 tbs. clarified butter
1 tsp. salt
2 tsp. mild paprika
2 pinches white pepper
1 cup pure, unsweetened apple juice
1¾ cup tomatoes
½ cup button mushrooms
2 tbs. chopped chives

Rinse chicken and cut into 8 pieces. • Peel onion, peel carrot and dice both. Wash white part of leeks and slice. • Heat 2 tbs. of the clarified butter in a large, heavy bottomed pan. Fry chicken pieces, turning as necessary to brown well on all sides, then remove from pan. • Brown diced onion and carrot in butter. Add remaining clarified butter and leeks, fry briefly, then lay chicken pieces on bed of vegetables. Sprinkle the mixture with salt, paprika and pepper before pouring on apple juice. Cover pan and cook over low heat for 35 minutes. • Skin tomatoes and chop, removing core. • Clean and rinse mushrooms, cut in fine slices and add with tomatoes to the stew for the final 10 minutes cooking time. • Serve stew sprinkled with chopped chives.

Chicken and Turnip Stew

Wholefood recipe, great value

550 calories per serving
Preparation time: 45 minutes
Cooking time: 1 hour, 25 minutes

Assorted soup vegetables (including carrot, celery, leek, onion)
1 chicken weighing 2½ lbs.
6 cups water
2 tsp. sea salt
5 white peppercorns
4½ cups turnips, preferably young white ones
1¼ cup shallots
Bunch parsley
2 pinches each, freshly ground black pepper and sea salt

Rinse, clean and finely dice soup vegetables. • Wash chicken thoroughly both inside and out. Put in pan with half the prepared soup vegetables, water, salt and peppercorns, and cook gently for 1 hour until tender. Remove any scum that forms during the first 30 minutes. • Peel and rinse turnips and cut in quarters lengthwise, then slice quarters thinly. Peel and halve shallots. • Remove chicken from broth. Cook turnips plus remaining soup vegetables and onions for 25 minutes in broth until done. Take meat off bones and cut in good sized pieces. • Rinse parsley in lukewarm water, dry well, remove thick stalks and chop leaves finely. • Remove pan from heat. Stir chicken meat and parsley into soup and season to taste with pepper and salt. • Serve with slices of hearty ryebread.

Chicken Stew with Mixed Vegetables

Worth the longer cooking time

900 calories per serving
Preparation time: 40 minutes
Cooking time: 2 hours, 10 minutes

2¼ cups carrots
1⅔ cups celery root
1¾ cup leeks
1 onion
2 cloves garlic
6 cups water
Sprig fresh thyme
1 bay leaf
1 clove
2 tsp. sea salt
1 tsp. white peppercorns
1 stewing chicken weighing 4 lbs.
2 kohlrabi (or young turnips)
1¾ cups zucchini
Pinch white pepper

Peel carrots and celery root, wash together with leeks. Roughly chop 2 carrots, celery root and 1 leek • Peel and dice onions and garlic. Bring prepared vegetables to a boil in the water together with thyme, bay leaf, clove, salt and peppercorns. • Rinse chicken and add to water, skimming off any scum that forms during the first 30 minutes. • Cook chicken gently 1½ hours longer until tender. • Remove green leaves from remaining leeks and slice. Cut peeled kohlrabi, rinsed zucchini and rest of carrots in julienne strips. • Remove chicken from broth. Strain broth, bring to a boil again and simmer vegetables in it for 10 minutes. • Separate meat from bones, cut in small cubes, return to pan and season to taste with salt and pepper.

Sweet and Sour Goose Giblets

Requires time

740 calories per serving
Soaking time: 12 hours
Preparation time: 25 minutes
Cooking time: 1 hour, 10 minutes

2 cups mixed dried fruit
2¼ lb. goose pieces (wings, neck, gizzard and heart)
3 cups water
1 onion
1 bay leaf
2 cloves
Soup vegetables (see index)
1 tsp. salt
¼ cup butter
5 tbs. flour
2 tbs. vinegar
1 tbs. sugar
2 pinches black pepper

Cover dried fruit with water and soak for 12 hours. • Rinse goose giblets, bring to a boil with the water and skim off scum as it forms. • Peel the onion and spike the bay leaf into it with the cloves. Clean and rinse soup vegetables, add to pan with onion and salt. Cover and cook 1 hour on gentle heat, when liquid should be reduced by one-third. • After 30 minutes of the cooking time, add dried fruit, along with the water it was soaked in. • Strain broth and measure out 2 cups. • Melt butter, brown flour in it, then gradually stir in broth and simmer for 10 minutes. • Season sauce with vinegar, sugar, salt and pepper. • Add dried fruit and chopped goose giblets to sauce and warm through. • Serve with bread dumplings.

Hungarian Chicken

Specialty from East Europe

810 calories per serving
Preparation time: 1 hour
Cooking time: 2 hours

1 stewing chicken weighing 3¼ lbs.
1½ tsp. salt
2 qts. water
Soup vegetables (see index)
¼ lb. bacon
4 medium onions
2 beefsteak tomatoes
2 green peppers
1 tbs. oil
2 tbs. mild paprika
Pinch each, salt and freshly ground white pepper

Wash chicken and giblets, putting liver to one side.

Bring to a boil with salt and water, removing scum as it forms. • Rinse and clean soup vegetables, add to chicken and cook 1½ hours. • Finely dice bacon and onions. Skin and chop tomatoes. Halve peppers, removing seeds and white ribs, before drying and cutting in strips. • Strain chicken broth and measure off 2 cups. Divide chicken into 12 portions and dice giblets. • Heat oil and fry bacon, then brown chicken pieces in bacon fat. Add onion and pepper and fry briefly. Stir in paprika and then chicken broth. Cook for 10 minutes. • Chop liver and add to pan with tomatoes, simmer gently for 10 minutes longer. Season to taste with salt and pepper.

Savoy Cabbage with Goose

Italian Specialty

950 calories per serving
Preparation time: 1 hour
Cooking time: 1½ hours

1 oz. bacon
3 medium carrots
2 onions
4½ cups Savoy cabbage
1 young fat goose weighing 6¾ lbs.
1 tbs. butter
½ cup full-bodied red wine
1 tsp. salt
2 pinches black pepper
1 tbs. tomato paste
½ cup chicken broth

Dice bacon. Peel and rinse carrots before slicing thinly. Peel onions, quarter them and cut in fine slices. • Cut cabbage in quarters, removing hard central core and any tough outer leaves. Rinse quarters and cut in thick slices. • Cut goose in 16 pieces, wash and dry them. • Preheat oven to 350°F. • Heat butter and bacon in a heavy bottomed casserole. Brown goose pieces thoroughly, add onions and carrots and continue to fry for 10 minutes more. Remove breast pieces and put to one side. • Add red wine, sliced cabbage, salt and pepper, mix well and fry a few minutes longer. • Combine tomato paste and chicken broth, pour over vegetables and cover casserole before placing in middle of oven. • Cook for 1½ hours, returning breast pieces to the dish for the last 30 minutes.

Turnip and Goose Stew

Economical and simple to prepare

790 calories per serving
Preparation and cooking time: 1½ hours
Cooking time: 50 minutes

1 goose carcass
1¼ lbs. roast goose
Gravy from roast
2 cups water
2 medium onions
2½ cups small white turnips
1¼ cups potatoes
1¼ cups carrots
½ cup goose or pork fat (saved from roasting goose)
1 tbs. flour
1 tsp. salt
Pinch freshly ground white pepper
2 tbs. freshly chopped parsley

Cut up goose carcass with poultry shears. Remove skin from meat. Cover carcass, skin and juices with the water and boil for 30 minutes, covered. • Peel and dice onions. Peel, wash and dice turnips, potatoes and carrots. Cut up cooked goose meat. • Strain goose broth. • Heat goose fat and fry onion till transparent; stir in flour and gradually add broth, stirring all the time. Add turnips to sauce, cover and cook for 20 minutes. • Add diced potato, carrots and salt and cook for 20 minutes longer. Add meat and heat with vegetables. Season stew with pepper and serve sprinkled with chopped parsley.

Cock-A-Leekie

Preparation requiring time, but economical

550 calories per serving
Preparation time: 40 minutes
Cooking time: 1½ hours

1 large onion
1 small chicken weighing 2¼ lbs. with heart and liver
10 prunes
6 tbs. pearl barley
1 tsp. salt
2 pinches freshly ground black pepper
3½ cups leeks
½ bunch parsley

Peel and dice onion. Wash chicken, put in pan with heart and prunes, barely cover with water and bring to a boil. Skim off scum as it forms. • Add diced onion, barley, salt and pepper to chicken, cover and simmer very gently for 1½ hours so that the surface of the water barely moves. • Cut off green leaves from leeks, halve lengthwise, wash thoroughly, dry and slice. • Add leek and liver to chicken after 1¼ hours and cook all together for last 15 minutes. • Remove cooked chicken from broth, skin it, take meat off bones and cut in fine strips, together with giblets. • In the meantime, continue to boil broth, uncovered, until reduced by one third. • Return meat to broth and season well with salt and pepper. • Wash and dry parsley, remove stalks and chop leaves before scattering over soup.

Waterzooi

Belgian specialty, quick and easy

690 calories per serving
Preparation time: 40 minutes
Cooking time: 1½ hours

7 oz. brisket of beef	
5 cups water	
2 tsp. salt	
6 allspice berries	
6 peppercorns	
1 small chicken weighing 2½ lbs.	
1 cup leeks	
1 cup carrots	
½ cup celery root	
1 onion	
2 tbs. butter	
2 tbs. flour	
2 egg yolks	
6 tbs. cream	
2 tsp. lemon juice	

Wash beef, bring to a boil with water, salt and spices, skimming off scum as it forms. Simmer gently for 45 minutes. • Cut chicken in half, rinse it with giblets, add to meat and cook 45 minutes longer. • Wash leeks, peel and rinse carrots, peel and rinse celery root, then chop them all. Peel and halve onion, add to soup with other prepared vegetables. Cook vegetables for last 30 minutes in soup. • Lift out beef and chicken and strain soup. Slice cooked carrots and leeks and dice celery root, discard onion. • Melt butter, add flour gradually add broth and simmer for a few minutes. • Remove chicken meat from carcass, cut up and return to soup with vegetables, putting beef and giblets aside to be used elsewhere. • Beat egg yolks with cream, thicken soup with this mixture and season to taste with salt and lemon juice.

Pasta and Chicken Stew

Fairly lengthy cooking time

500 calories per serving
Preparation time: 50 minutes
Cooking time: 1 hour, 35 minutes

1 roasting chicken weighing 2¼ lbs.	
6 cups water	
1 tsp. salt	
3 allspice berries	
3 peppercorns	
½ bay leaf	
Soup vegetables (see index)	
1 onion	
2 cloves garlic	
2 cups each, eggplant, zucchini and small tomatoes	
Sprig thyme	
1 tbs. oil	
½ cup pasta for soup	

Wash chicken and giblets, bring to a boil with water, salt, spices and bay leaf. Skim off scum as it forms. • Poach chicken 1½ hours in uncovered pan, allowing the surface of the liquid to scarcely move. • Wash, clean and chop soup vegetables, and add to chicken at the end of the first half hour. • Peel and dice onion and garlic. Wash, dry and dice eggplant and zucchini. • Skin and dice tomatoes, removing core. Rinse thyme. • Heat oil; fry onion and garlic until transparent. Add diced vegetables and thyme, continuing to fry for 10 minutes longer. • Strain chicken broth, adding one cup to vegetables. Bring remaining broth to a boil, add pasta and boil for 5 minutes. • Take chicken meat off carcass, cut up and add to vegetables. Pour cooked pasta and remaining broth over the mixture and combine.

Country Stew

Quick and easy

380 calories per serving
Preparation time: 1 hour
Cooking time: 45 minutes

1¾ lbs. boned turkey thighs	
1 onion	
1 bay leaf	
2 cloves	
2–3 cups water	
½ tsp. salt	
2 carrots	
2 leeks	
1 cup heavy cream	
2 tbs. freshly grated horseradish	

Wash and dry meat. Peel onion and use the cloves to spike the bay leaf onto it. • Bring water to a boil. Add salt, onion and turkey; boil for 45 minutes. Skim off any scum that forms during the first 20 minutes. • Peel, wash and slice carrots. Remove root end and dark green leaves from leeks, split in two lengthwise before washing thoroughly, and chop in ¾ in. pieces. • When turkey has been cooking for 20 minutes, add prepared vegetables and continue to cook in covered pan. • Whip cream lightly and stir in horseradish. • Arrange meat and vegetables in a tureen, discarding onion. Serve horseradish cream separately. Good accompanied by rye bread.

Paella

Spanish specialty requiring time for successful preparation

625 calories per serving
Preparation and cooking time: 1 hour 15 minutes

1 chicken weighing 2½ lbs.
9 oz. pork tenderloin
1 tsp. salt
2 pinches freshly ground black pepper
6 tbs. olive oil
1 lb. 2 oz. mussels
6 jumbo shrimp
1¼ cup long grain rice
9 oz. chorizos or similar highly seasoned smoked pork
Sausages
2 onions
2 cloves garlic
3 cups meat bouillon
½ cup dry white wine
3 pinches saffron
1 cup shelled green peas
4 beefsteak tomatoes
½ cup black olives
1 organically grown lemon

Wash chicken inside and out, dry and cut in 12 pieces. Wash and dry pork tenderloin and cut in ¾ in. cubes. • Season chicken and pork with salt and pepper. • Heat ½ cup of the oil in a large skillet and brown chicken pieces thoroughly. Add cubed pork and brown it in the same way, then reduce heat and fry for 20 minutes longer, turning the meat frequently. • Wash and scrub mussels, removing beards. Peel shrimp and make a shallow cut along center back to devein. • Rinse rice several times until water runs clear, then drain. Slice sausages and fry briefly with the meat. • Peel and finely chop onions and

garlic, and brown in remaining oil in a large pan. Add rice, fry for a short time with onions before pouring on stock and white wine. Stir in saffron. Boil rice gently on low heat for 10 minutes. • Add peas and cook 10 minutes longer. • Cut a shallow cross in rounded side of tomatoes, immerse in boiling water and remove skin. Cut in 8 pieces, taking out core. • Preheat oven to 400°F. Spread the rice in the bottom of a paella pan or a large, flat ovenware dish. Arrange the pieces of chicken, pork and sausage, prepared mussels, prawns and tomato on the rice. Place uncovered in oven and cook for 20 minutes. • Rinse olives under cold running water, dry and halve, removing pits. Wash lemon in hot water, dry and cut in 8 segments. • Allow cooked paella to stand for 5 minutes in oven once it has been switched off, then scatter olives

over the top, garnish with wedges of lemon and serve at once.

Variations: In Spain, paella is prepared in different ways according to region and what is available at the local market. In coastal areas, squid and various types of fish are used. Anyone who brings back genuine chorizos from a trip to Spain can prepare an authentic paella.

Southern Chicken Stew

Specialty requiring some time in the preparation

570 calories per serving
Preparation time: 45 minutes
Cooking time: 1½ hours

1 small stewing chicken weighing 2½ lbs.
2 tsp. salt
1 onion
3 medium potatoes
1¾ cup tomatoes
Small can kidney beans (7 oz.)
Small can sweet corn kernels (7 oz.)
Sugar
1 tsp. salt
2 pinches freshly ground white pepper
2 tbs. finely chopped chives

Wash chicken and cut in 8 pieces, then place in pan with giblets and boiling water to just cover. • Simmer on low heat without the lid for 45 minutes, removing scum as necessary. • Next add salt, cover pan with lid and cook chicken gently for 45 minutes more. • Peel onion and cut in rings. Scrub potatoes thoroughly under running warm water, then peel, rinse and coarsely dice. Add to chicken, together with onion, for the final 20 minutes of cooking time. • Make crosswise cuts through the skin on the round side of tomatoes, plunge briefly into boiling water, then remove skin and core. Cut in segments. Add tomatoes, drained kidney beans and sweet corn to chicken and cook together for last 10 minutes of cooking time. • Remove chicken from stew, separate meat from skin and bones, then cut in pieces and return to stew. Season with sugar, salt and pepper, then reheat. Sprinkle with chopped chives before serving.

Caucasian Chicken Stew

Economical, Russian specialty

570 calories per serving
Preparation time: 30 minutes
Cooking time: 45 minutes

1 chicken weighing 2¼ lbs.
½ tsp. salt
½ tsp. mild paprika
Pinch freshly ground black pepper
¼ cup oil
1 small onion
1 cup celery root
1 carrot
¾ cup cucumber
¾ cup pumpkin (or zucchini, if unavailable)
1 cup long grain rice
1 bay leaf
Pinch ground fennel seed
4 cups water
1 gerkhin pickle
¼ cup sour cream

Wash and dry chicken, then quarter it. • Mix salt, paprika and pepper with 1 tbs. of the oil. Coat chicken pieces with this mixture and marinate for 10 minutes. • Peel onion and celery root, peel carrot, and rinse all three. Peel cucumber and pumpkin. Cut vegetables in 1¼ in. pieces. • Heat remaining oil in a large, flame-proof casserole. Sauté chicken, then add vegetables (except cucumber and pumpkin) and fry all together. • Wash rice, add it to chicken with bay leaf and fennel, pour on water, cover and cook gently on low heat for 30 minutes. • Preheat oven to 475°F. • Add cubed cucumber and pumpkin to rice mixture. Place casserole, uncovered, in middle of oven and cook for 15 minutes. • Finely chop gerkhin and stir into sour cream. • Serve Caucasian Stew straight from the dish, with an island of cream floating in the middle.

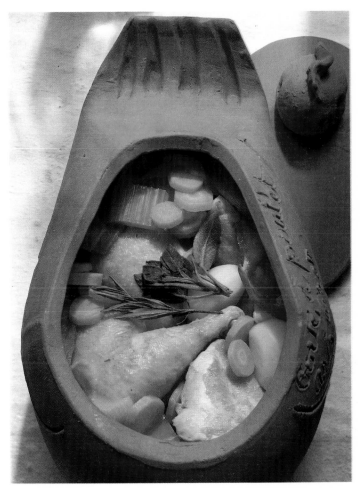

Chicken in a Roman Pot

Italian specialty

640 calories per serving
Preparation time: 25 minutes
Cooking time: 1½ hours

2¼ cups celery
1¾ carrots
1¾ cup small potatoes
1 roasting chicken weighing 2½ lbs.
1 tbs. lemon juice
1 tsp. salt
½ tsp. freshly ground white pepper
2 oz. thinly sliced bacon
5 tbs. dry white wine
Sprig fresh rosemary
2 sage leaves
1 tbs. butter

Soak Roman pot and lid for about 20 minutes in cold water. • Wash celery, remove strings and cut in 1¼ in. lengths. Peel, wash and dry carrots; slice. Peel and wash potatoes, then quarter them. • Cut chicken in 8 equal pieces, wash these and dry before sprinkling with lemon juice. • Season with salt and pepper, rubbing in well. • Take brick out of water and line with bacon slices. Arrange one half of vegetables in it, season lightly with salt and pepper. Lay chicken pieces on top and finish with rest of vegetables, seasoning lightly again. • Sprinkle wine over vegetables. Wash and dry herbs before laying them on top. • Put lid on pot and place in bottom of cold oven. Cook chicken 1½ hours at 425°F. • Remove lid 10 minutes before end of cooking time and dab small pieces of butter over vegetables.

Creamy Asparagus and Chicken

More expensive but easy to prepare

360 calories per serving
Preparation and cooking time: 1 hour

5¼ cups asparagus
2 qts. water
1 tsp. salt
1 lb. 2 oz. boned chicken breast, skinned
1 tbs. clarified butter
1 tbs. butter
2 heaping tbs. flour
½ cup milk
Good pinch each, salt and freshly ground white pepper
1 egg yolk
5 tbs. sour cream
2 tbs. chopped chives

Peel ends of asparagus. Bring water and salt to a boil, put in asparagus and boil for about 15 minutes, until cooked but still firm. • Wash and dry chicken pieces, cut in 1¼ in. cubes and sauté for 6 minutes in clarified butter. Remove cubes from pan. • Drain asparagus, putting aside 1 cup of the cooking water. • Melt butter in a pan, sprinkle in flour, continue cooking until it turns slightly brown, then add milk gradually to form a creamy sauce. Season to taste with salt and pepper, then simmer gently, stirring continuously, for 10 minutes. • Cut asparagus in 1½ in. lengths and add to sauce with cubed chicken. • Beat egg yolk with sour cream, stir into sauce, remove from heat and sprinkle with chives.

Garbure Bearnaise

Specialty from France

500 calories per serving
Preparation time: 30 minutes
Cooking time: 1 hour 50 minutes

| 2 goose leg pieces, weighing 1¼ lbs. each |
| 4¼ cups water |
| 1 tsp. salt |
| 1 onion |
| ½ bay leaf |
| ½ cup carrots |
| 1 cup white turnips |
| 1 cup potatoes |
| 1 cup white cabbage |
| 1 cup green beans |
| 6 oz. canned white beans |
| 2 sprigs chervil |
| Sprig lovage |
| Pinch white pepper |
| 4 tbs. grated mild cheddar cheese |
| 1 tbs. chopped parsley |

Wash goose and bring to a boil with water and salt. Peel onion and add to pan with bay leaf. Cook about 20 minutes, uncovered, removing scum as it forms. • Cover and simmer gently for 1 hour more. • Peel carrots and turnips before washing and dicing them. Peel potatoes and dice, not too finely. • Prepare cabbage, rinse leaves and shred. Wash and chop green beans. • Add all prepared vegetables, together with drained white beans, herbs and pepper to pan. Cover and simmer for 30 minutes. • Remove goose from pan and cut meat off bones, cut in cubes and return to pan. Sprinkle finished dish with cheese and parsley.

Soljanka

Specialty from Russia

550 calories per serving
Preparation time: 30 minutes
Cooking time: 2 hours

| 1 small chicken weighing 2½ lbs. |
| Soup vegetables |
| 1 onion |
| 6 cups water |
| 2 tsp. salt |
| 2 allspice berries |
| 2½ cups white cabbage |
| 2 gherkin pickles |
| ½ cup dry white wine |
| 2 pinches freshly ground white pepper |
| 6 tbs. sour cream |
| 3 tbs. fresh dill |

Wash chicken and giblets. • Clean and rinse soup vegetables, then coarsely chop. Peel and halve onion. • Bring water to a boil with salt and allspice berries. Put in chicken, onion and soup vegetables. Cook uncovered for 30 minutes, skimming off scum as it forms. Almost cover pan with lid and continue to cook chicken for 1 hour more. • Clean and rinse white cabbage and shred coarsely. Cut pickles in julienne strips, add both to pan and cover completely before continuing to cook. • Take chicken from pan, remove meat from carcass and cut in pieces. • Boil soup uncovered, until reduced by half. Return chicken meat to soup, add wine and season to taste with pepper. Stir sour cream into soup. • Sprinkle with dill before serving.

Creole Jambalaya

Specialty from the U.S.A.

550 calories per serving
Preparation time: 45 minutes
Cooking time: 55 minutes

7 oz. smoked pork tenderloin
1 chicken weighing 2½ lbs.
1 tsp. salt
Pinch white pepper
5 tbs. oil
2 onions
1 clove garlic
2 green and 1 red pepper
2 beefsteak tomatoes
3 cups hot chicken bouillon
2 cups long grain rice
2 pinches cayenne pepper
2 pinches saffron
7 oz. smoked garlic sausage
7 oz. lean ham
7 oz. cooked lobster meat

W ash and pat dry pork and chicken, cutting pork in ¾ in. cubes and chicken in 8 pieces. • Mix salt and pepper and oil, pour over combined pork and chicken, cover and leave to marinate for 30 minutes. • Peel and dice onions and garlic. Halve peppers, remove seeds, ribs and stems before rinsing, drying and dicing. Skin and chop tomatoes. • Brown meat in a large, heavy bottomed pan. Add diced onion, garlic and peppers, fry all together before pouring on half the bouillon. Cover and simmer for 30 minutes. • Add tomatoes, washed rice, remaining bouillon, cayenne pepper and saffron to meat, mixing in well, and continue to simmer for 20 minutes more. • Slice sausage, cut ham and lobster in strips. Lay on top of rice combination, heat through for 5 minutes.

Chicken Pot-Au-Feu

Economical specialty from France

500 calories per serving
Preparation time: 35 minutes
Cooking time: 1 hour

1 chicken weighing 2½ lbs.	
3 cups chicken bouillon	
½ cup carrots	
1 cup leeks	
1 large onion	
2¼ cups sauerkraut	
1 bay leaf	
4 juniper berries	
1¾ cup tomatoes	
½ tsp. each, salt and freshly ground black pepper	

Wash chicken, heart and liver, dry them and divide chicken into 8 pieces. • Bring chicken bouillon to a boil in a large casserole. Put chicken pieces and heart into stock, lower the heat and cook uncovered for 30 minutes. Skim off any scum that forms. • Peel, rinse and dice carrots. Cut white part of leeks in 2 in. lengths, split these in half and wash. Peel onion and slice in rings. Roughly chop sauerkraut and combine with bay leaf and juniper berries. • Add all prepared vegetables and chicken liver to broth, cover and simmer for 30 minutes. • Make crosswise cuts in the rounded end of tomatoes, cover with boiling water, skin and cut in segments, removing any core. • Add prepared tomatoes to casserole 10 minutes before end of cooking time; season well with salt and pepper. • Serve with hot French bread.

Chicken Drumsticks with Lentils

Economical, quick and easy

880 calories per serving
Preparation time: 25 minutes
Cooking time: 45 minutes

2¼ cups lentils	
6½ cups water	
1 cup dry red wine	
4 chicken drumsticks weighing approx. 7 oz. each	
1 chicken bouillon cube	
1 bay leaf	
1 dried chili	
Pinch freshly ground white pepper	
½ tsp. dried thyme	
1 tsp. dried basil	
¼ lb. bacon	
1 tbs. oil	
2 onions	
1 clove garlic	
Good pinch each, sugar and salt	
2 tbs. freshly chopped parsley	

Wash lentils several times in a bowl of water, then cover with the water and red wine and bring to a boil. • Wash drumsticks and add to lentils together with crumbled bouillon cube. Add bay leaf, chili, pepper, thyme and basil; bring to a boil again and simmer, covered, on gentle heat for 45 minutes. • Cut bacon into small squares and fry in oil. Peel onions and slice in rings before frying to a golden brown in bacon fat. Peel and crush garlic and mix with onions. • Scatter onion mixture over lentils. • Season to taste with salt and sugar before serving sprinkled with chopped parsley.

Turkey Liver Pilaff

Simple to make

500 calories per serving
Preparation time: 45 minutes
Cooking time: 50 minutes

1 cup long grain rice	
3 cups water	
1 tsp. salt	
1 lb. 2 oz. turkey livers	
1 large onion	
2 red peppers	
2 tbs. clarified butter	
½ cup vegetable bouillon	
¼ cup white wine	
Pinch each, salt and freshly ground white pepper	
¼ cup sour cream	
1 tbs. chopped parsley	

Wash rice in sieve under running water until it runs clear. Bring water and salt to a boil, add rice, cover, turn heat low and leave to absorb liquid for about 20 minutes. • Wash and dry turkey livers, then cut in ¾ in. cubes. Peel and finely dice onions. Halve red peppers, remove stems, ribs and seeds before rinsing and chopping in small pieces. • Heat 1 tbs. of the clarified butter in a heavy bottomed pan, fry turkey livers for 4 minutes, then remove from pan and keep warm. • Put remaining clarified butter in pan with diced onion and fry until transparent. Add chopped peppers and fry for 10 minutes longer. Pour in vegetable bouillon, cover and steam vegetables for 10 minutes. • Mix in rice, white wine and cooked liver. Season with salt and pepper, and stir in sour cream and parsley.

Fricassees
and
Ragoûts

Braised Pigeons with Chocolate Sauce

A Spanish specialty and rather more expensive

520 calories per serving
Preparation time: 40 minutes
Cooking time: 50 minutes

2 cloves garlic
4 pigeons weighing 1 lb. 2 oz. each
1 tsp. salt
2 pinches freshly ground white pepper
3 tbs. flour
¼ cup olive oil
¼ cup dry white wine
1 cup chicken bouillon
1 cup shallots
2 oz. cooking chocolate

Peel and finely chop the garlic. • Wash pigeons inside and out, then dry and rub with salt and pepper, inside and out. Toss in 2 tbs. of the flour. • Heat oil in large, heavy bottomed pan and brown pigeons on all sides. Fry garlic in remaining oil. Stir rest of flour into oil, fry briefly, then add wine and chicken bouillon. Simmer for 5 minutes, stirring constantly. • Put pigeons into sauce, cover and cook for 50 minutes on a low heat. • Peel shallots, dice finely and add to pigeons after 30 minutes. • Preheat oven to 225°F. • Arrange cooked pigeons on a serving dish and keep hot in oven. • Skim fat off sauce. Grate chocolate and add to sauce, stirring continuously over a low heat until melted. Do not let the sauce boil again. Season generously with salt and pepper and serve with pigeons. • To accompany this dish, serve either rice, cooked until tender, or crisp French bread, plus a fresh mixed salad.

Coq Au Vin

930 calories per serving
Preparation time: 50 minutes
Cooking time: 50 minutes

1 chicken weighing 3¼ lbs.	
½ tsp. salt	
Pinch white pepper	
¼ lb. bacon, in 1 piece	
8 small onions	
1 clove garlic	
2 carrots	
2 tbs. clarified butter	
1 bay leaf	
1 sprig thyme	
2 sprigs parsley	
3 cups dry red wine	
¾ cup button mushrooms	
½ bunch flat leaved parsley	
1 tsp. flour	
2 tbs. brandy	

Wash and dry chicken, cut in 8 pieces and season with salt and pepper. Finely dice bacon, peel and chop onions and garlic. Clean, wash and dice carrots. • Heat clarified butter in a heavy bottomed pan and brown chicken pieces and bacon. Add chopped onion and garlic with rest of prepared vegetables and continue to fry. • Add bay leaf, thyme and parsley sprigs with red wine. Cook chicken for 40 minutes. • Wash and dice mushrooms. • Remove chicken from pan and keep warm. Rub vegetables with cooking juices through a sieve, then simmer mushrooms in this sauce for 10 minutes. • Wash and chop parsley • Thicken sauce with flour mixed to a paste with cold water. Season to taste with salt and brandy, then pour over chicken. Sprinkle with parsley. • White bread should accompany this dish.

Coq Au Riesling

Specialty from Alsace

980 calories per serving
Preparation time: 30 minutes
Cooking time: 35 minutes

1 chicken weighing 3¼ lbs.	
¾ cup shallots	
1 tsp. salt	
2 cloves garlic	
½ bunch fresh tarragon	
¼ cup butter	
½ tsp. freshly ground white pepper	
2 tbs. chopped parsley	
2 cups Alsatian Riesling (white wine)	
1 cup button mushrooms	
½ tsp. flour	
1 cup sour cream	

Cut wings off chicken. Peel and quarter shallots. Put 1 shallot, together with wings, some salt and 1 cup water, in a pan and boil for 20 minutes. Strain broth. • Wash and dry chicken, then cut in 8 pieces. Peel and chop garlic. Rinse and finely chop tarragon. • Heat half the butter and brown chicken pieces. Add pepper, salt, shallots, garlic, herbs, wine and broth. Cook chicken for 25 minutes. • Rinse mushrooms, slice thinly, sprinkle with flour and brown in remaining butter. • Remove lid from pan, increase heat and continue to cook chicken another 10 minutes until done. • Lift out chicken pieces and keep warm. Stir sour cream into sauce together with mushrooms. Season to taste with salt and pepper and pour over chicken.

Pigeons with Bulgur Wheat Stuffing

Specialty from Egypt

570 calories per serving
Preparation time: 25 minutes
Cooking time: 30 minutes

| 4 young pigeons weighing 9 oz. each |
| 1 bunch scallions |
| ¼ cup butter |
| ½ cup cracked wheat (bulgur wheat) |
| ½ tbs. freshly chopped mint |
| 1 tsp. salt |
| ½ tsp. freshly ground white pepper |
| 3 cups chicken bouillon |

Wash and dry pigeons and giblets. Finely chop giblets. • Clean, rinse and chop scallions, combine with giblets and brown in 1 tbs. of the butter. Add cracked wheat and chopped mint, season stuffing with salt and pepper. • Rub insides of pigeons with salt and fill each with 2 tbs. of wheat mixture. Sew cavity openings together. • Preheat oven to 425°F. • Put pigeons in roaster. Melt remaining butter and trickle over pigeons. Pour 2 cups of the chicken bouillon into pan and bring to a boil on the burner. • Roast pigeons for 30 minutes in oven, basting frequently with liquid. • Meanwhile, bring remaining bouillon to a boil, add rest of cracked wheat mixture to it and stand over low heat for 30 minutes to allow wheat to absorb liquid. Spoon onto warm serving dish and arrange pigeons on top.

Braised Quails

Specialty from Lebanon demanding skill in preparation

740 calories per serving
Preparation time: 1½ hours
Cooking time: 20 minutes

| 8 quails weighing ¼ lb. each |
| 1 tsp. salt |
| ½ tsp. white pepper |
| 8 thin slices bacon (¼ lb.) |
| ¼ cup oil |
| ½ cup white raisins |
| 3 medium onions |
| 4 allspice berries |
| ⅓ cup sweet white wine (Sauterne) |
| 1 clove garlic |
| ½ cup long grain rice |
| 3 cups chicken bouillon |
| 2 pinches saffron |

Wash and dry quails and season with salt and pepper. Wrap a slice of bacon around each and tie securely with kitchen thread. • Heat 2 tbs. of the oil in a heavy bottomed pan, brown quails for 10 minutes then take them out and keep warm. • Wash and drain white raisins. Peel and chop onions; brown two-thirds of them in oil left in the pan. Add white raisins, allspice berries and white wine with an equal quantity of water to pan, bring to a boil and season to taste with salt. Simmer sauce gently for 20 minutes on low heat, then strain. • Cook quails for 20 minutes in sauce. • Peel and chop garlic, then fry with remaining onion in 2 tbs. oil. Add washed rice, chicken bouillon and saffron to pan and cook all together for 20 minutes.

Turkey and Curd Cheese Roulades

Easy to prepare

380 calories per serving
Preparation time: 30 minutes
Cooking time: 20 minutes

2 medium carrots
1 small onion
3 tbs. clarified butter
2 tbs. chopped mixed herbs (e.g. dill, chervil, thyme, parsley, lemon balm)
½ cup full cream curd cheese or cream cheese
1 egg yolk
1 tbs. mustard
Pinch each, salt and freshly ground white pepper
4 turkey cutlets (sliced thin) weighing 6 oz. each
1 cup hot chicken bouillon
¼ cup dry vermouth
2 tbs. sour cream

Peel and rinse carrots before cutting in julienne strips. Peel and dice onion. • Heat 1 tbs. of the clarified butter. Saute prepared onion and carrot on low heat for 5 minutes, then cool slightly. • Mix herbs with cream cheese, egg yolk, mustard, salt and pepper. • Wash and dry turkey cutlets, then spread with herb and cheese mixture. Divide cooled vegetables evenly between the cutlets and spread on top of cheese. Roll meat up and fasten with toothpicks. • Heat remaining clarified butter and brown roulades thoroughly over moderate heat. Add chicken bouillon and vermouth; cover and simmer for 20 minutes over low heat till done • Stir sour cream into cooking juices. Serve with parsley potatoes.

Turkey and Vegetable Roulades

Quick and easy

570 calories per serving
Preparation time: 45 minutes
Cooking time: 45 minutes

½ cup raisins
¼ lb. raw ham
1 bunch parsley
2 tbs. pine kernels
1 tbs. capers
4 turkey cutlets (sliced thin) weighing 6 oz. each
4 pinches each, salt and freshly ground white pepper
1 onion
¼ cup olive oil
1 can tomato paste (3 oz.)
½ cup water
1 cup cream
1 small bay leaf
3 rosemary leaves
Pinch dried thyme
1 red pepper
Pinch sugar

Cover raisins with water and bring to a boil. • Cube ham. Wash, dry and chop parsley. Drain raisins, mix with ham, parsley, pine kernels and capers. • Wash and dry turkey cutlets, sprinkle with salt and pepper. Spread meat with filling, roll up and fasten with toothpicks. • Peel and chop onion. • Heat oil. Brown roulades thoroughly, then add chopped onion and dry briefly with meat. Add tomato paste with water, cream, bay leaf and other herbs. Simmer roulades for 20 minutes. • Clean, wash and dry red pepper, cut in strips and cook for last 10 minutes with meat. Season sauce with sugar to taste.

Hungarian Turkey Ragout

Quick and easy to prepare

330 calories per serving
Preparation time: 30 minutes
Cooking time: 30 minutes

1 lb. 2 oz. turkey breast
1 onion
1¼ cup button mushrooms
1 tbs. lemon juice
2 tbs. oil
1 tbs. butter
½ cup sour cream
1 tsp. cornstarch
1 tsp. milk paprika
½ cup dry white wine
½ tsp. each, salt and freshly ground white pepper

Wash and dry meat before cutting in thin slices. • Peel and finely chop onion. Wash and clean mushrooms, slice thinly and sprinkle with lemon juice. • Heat oil in a large, heavy bottomed pan. Brown meat, turning until done, then remove from pan. • Melt butter with oil in pan and fry onion until transparent. Add mushrooms, cover and sauté for 10 minutes. • Mix sour cream with cornstarch and paprika. • Return meat to pan with mushrooms, add cream mixture and then white wine. Simmer ragout gently for a few minutes. • Season to taste with salt and pepper. • Potato croquettes or noodles with a fresh green salad go well with this dish.

Turkey Liver with Banana Rice

Quick and easy

640 calories per serving
Preparation time: 35 minutes
Cooking time: 20 minutes

1 cup long grain rice
2½ qts. water
1 tsp. salt
1¼ lbs. turkey liver
1 tbs. flour
½ cup shallots
3 tbs. butter
3 tbs. curry powder
¼ cup slivered almonds
½ cup cream
½ cup chicken bouillon
2 pinches white pepper
2 small bananas
1 tsp. lemon juice

Wash rice in sieve under running water till water runs clear. • Bring water and salt to a boil. Pour rice into rapidly-boiling water and continue to boil for 20 minutes. • Wash liver carefully and dry, cut into even pieces and dust with flour. • Peel and finely chop shallots. • Melt 2 tbs. of the butter in a large, heavy bottomed pan and fry shallots until transparent. Add liver and continue to fry for 5 minutes, turning continuously. Sprinkle 2 tbs. of the curry powder and slivered almonds over liver, add cream and chicken bouillon, then simmer very gently over low heat for 5 minutes. Season to taste with salt and pepper. • Drain rice in a sieve. • Peel and slice bananas before browning in remaining butter. Mix remaining curry powder and rice with banana slices, adding lemon juice to taste. • Serve ragout with banana rice.

Chicken Liver and Lentils

Economical and quick to make

430 calories per serving
Preparation time: 40 minutes
Cooking time: 20 minutes

4¼ cups water	
1¾ cups red lentils	
¼ lb. raw ham without fat	
1 lb. 2 oz. chicken livers	
1 bunch parsley	
½ bunch sage	
¼ cup butter	
1 tbs. olive oil	
3 tbs. chicken bouillon	
1 tsp. salt	
2 pinches black pepper	

Bring water to a boil and cook lentils over low heat for 8 minutes, then drain in sieve. • Finely dice ham. Wash livers in cold water, dry, remove any fat or skin and cut in strips. • Wash, dry and, finely chop parsley and sage. • Heat half the butter with oil in a large pan. Fry ham and herbs over low heat, stirring, then add chicken bouillon. Cover and continue to cook for 5 minutes longer. • Heat remaining butter, fry chicken livers for 3–4 minutes, turning constantly. Season with salt and pepper, mix with lentils and serve immediately. • Mashed potatoes or hot French bread should accompany this dish.

Tip: Chicken livers may be combined with sweet corn or peas instead of the lentils used here.

Chicken Liver in Yogurt Sauce

Quick and good value

330 calories per serving
Preparation time: 35 minutes
Cooking time: 35 minutes

1 bunch each parsley, basil and chives	
1¼ cups full cream yogurt	
¼ cup cream	
1 tsp. lemon juice	
1 clove garlic	
Pinch each salt, white pepper and sugar	
1 lb. 2 oz. chicken livers	
2 medium onions	
3 tbs. oil	
1 tbs. flour	
½ tsp. dried mixed herbs	
Pinch salt	
2 pinches freshly ground black pepper	

Wash and dry herbs and chop finely. Mix yogurt with cream, lemon juice and herbs. Peel and chop garlic, sprinkle with salt and crush before adding to yogurt mixture. Season to taste with pepper and sugar. • Remove any fat or skin from chicken livers, wash and dry. • Peel onions and cut in thin rings. Heat 1 tbs. of the oil in a skillet, brown onion rings for about 5 minutes, then remove from pan. • Heat remaining oil in skillet. Roll liver in flour and dry in small amounts for about 2 minutes until brown. Sprinkle with herbs. Finally, add fried onions to liver, continue to fry for 1 minute longer, season to taste with salt and pepper before serving with yogurt sauce. • Potatoes boiled in their skins are best with this dish.

Chicken Hearts with Vegetables

Requires time in preparation

520 calories per serving
Preparation time: 1 hour
Cooking time: 20 minutes

2¼ lb. chicken hearts	
1 onion	
2 stalks celery	
1¼ cups each, small carrots, shallot and potatoes	
¼ cup olive oil	
½ cup dry white wine	
1 cup chicken bouillon	
2 pinches salt	
Pinch freshly ground black pepper	
1 bunch parsley	

S lice hearts in half, cutting off any fat. Wash hearts, removing any remaining blood, and dry. • Peel and roughly chop onion. Remove coarse strings from celery, wash and slice thinly. Peel carrots, wash and cut in rounds. Peel and dice shallots and potatoes. • Heat 3 tbs. of the oil in a heavy bottomed pan. Fry onion until transparent, then add hearts and continue to fry until they turn light gray. Pour in white wine and allow to evaporate while stirring continuously. • Stir in vegetables and chicken bouillon, season to taste with salt and pepper. Cook hearts gently on low heat until they are tender, about 15 minutes. • Mix in remaining oil. Wash, dry and chop parsley, then sprinkle over the finished dish.

Turkey Liver and Tomato

A quick and economical dish

310 calories per serving
Preparation time: 40 minutes

2 large onions	
3 ripe beefsteak tomatoes	
¼ cup butter	
½ cup dry white wine	
1⅛ lbs. turkey liver	
1 tsp. flour	
½ tsp. salt	
2 sprigs sage	
2 pinches freshly ground black pepper	

P eel onions and slice in rings. Cut a shallow cross in rounded end of tomatoes, immerse briefly in boiling water, then skin and cut in segments, removing core. • Heat 2 tbs. butter in frying pan, brown onions, pour in white wine and cover, then simmer about 5 minutes until done. • Add tomato segments to onion, cook on medium heat 5 minutes longer, uncovered, to thicken liquid slightly. • Wash and pat dry turkey livers, removing any fat or skin. Cut in strips and dust with flour. • Wash and dry sage. • Heat remaining butter in another pan and fry liver strips until they turn gray. • Add cooked liver to tomato sauce, seasoning with salt and pepper, and sprinkling with sage leaves. Serve hot, preferably with parsley potatoes.

Tip: Cooked rice may be added to the finished dish, provided some chicken broth has been added to the sauce.

Poultry Liver with Celery

Simple to prepare

670 calories per serving
Preparation time: 1 hour

1½ lbs. poultry liver
1 tbs. flour
3 tbs. olive oil
1 onion
1 can skinned tomatoes
2 large beefsteak tomatoes
2½ cups celery
½ tsp. salt
Pinch freshly ground white pepper
1 tsp. dried oregano
1 cup walnut pieces
1 cup sour cream
½ bunch lemon balm

Wash and pat dry livers, remove any skin or fat and cut in pieces. • Dust liver with flour, brown well on all sides in olive oil and remove from pan. • Peel and finely chop onion before frying until transparent in remaining oil. • Drain canned tomatoes, rub through sieve and add purée to onion. Simmer to allow sauce to thicken slightly. • Make a shallow cross in tomato skins, cover with boiling water, skin and cut in segments, removing hard core. • Pull off celery string, then wash sticks and chop in 1 in. pieces. Add prepared tomatoes and celery to tomato purée Cover and simmer vegetables for 15 minutes, then season with salt, pepper and oregano. • Wash and dry lemon balm leaves. Chop walnuts and add to vegetables with liver and sour cream. Reheat fricassee, then sprinkle with lemon balm. • Serve with mashed potato.

Chicken Curry

Quick but more expensive

260 calories per serving
Preparation time: 30 minutes

1⅛ lbs. chicken breast fillets
½ bunch spring onions
1 large beefsteak tomato
½ pineapple (approx. 1 lb.)
2 tbs. clarified butter
1 tsp. flour
2 tbs. curry powder
1 cup chicken broth
1 tsp. lemon juice
Pinch salt

Wash and dry meat and cut in ½ in. wide strips. • Chop dark green ends off spring onions; wash and dry, then chop light green parts in ½ in. rings, slice white ends in 4, lengthwise. • Core tomato with sharp knife.

Cover with boiling water, skin and chop. • Divide pineapple in 8, cut away hard core, loosen flesh from skin and cut across in thin slices. • Heat clarified butter and brown chicken. Add onions and chopped tomato, fry 1 minute longer. • Combine flour and curry powder, then stir into fricassee. Add chicken broth slowly, stirring well. • Add pineapple pieces and heat gently for 5 minutes. Season curry to taste with lemon juice and salt. • Serve with rice cooked until tender.

Fricassee with Walnuts

Quick but rather expensive

430 calories per serving
Preparation time: 35 minutes

1⅛ lbs. chicken breast fillets
3 tbs. soy sauce
2 tbs. dry sherry
½ tsp. sugar
Pinch salt
2 tbs. cornflour
1 red pepper
1 medium onion
1 cup celery
5 tbs. oil
1 cup walnut halves
½ cup hot chicken broth

Wash and dry meat; cut in 1 in. cubes. • Mix soy sauce, sherry, sugar, salt and cornflour together and combine with meat.

• Remove stem, ribs and seeds from red pepper; wash and dry, then cut in strips. Peel and halve onion; cut in strips. String celery, wash and dry, then cut in julienne strips. • Heat 1 tbs. oil and brown walnut halves, then remove from pan. • Add 1 tbs. oil to pan and brown celery, then onion and pepper, one minute each, over high heat. Take vegetables out of pan. • Heat remaining oil in pan, fry chicken cubes for 3 minutes, turning frequently. Turn heat down and pour on chicken broth. Heat vegetables and walnuts briefly in fricassee. Serve with rice.

Light Chicken Fricassee

Requires certain amount of time

760 calories per serving
Preparation time: 30 minutes
Cooking time: 1 hour

1 chicken weighing 3¼ lbs.
1 bay leaf
2 onions
1 tsp. each, salt and peppercorns
Pinch white pepper
Soup vegetables
2 tbs. butter
½ cup dry white wine
1 cup cream
1 cup sour cream
1 cup carrots
¾ cup celery
1 small kohlrabi
1 small leek
½ tsp. dried tarragon
1 tbs. chopped parsley

Remove legs and breast from chicken. Cut rest of bird in several pieces, put in pot with bay leaf, 1 washed but unpeeled onion, salt, peppercorns and about 4 cups water. Bring to a boil and cook uncovered for 30 minutes, until liquid is reduced to about 1 cup. • Sieve chicken broth. Keep cooked meat to use elsewhere. Wash, dry and halve chicken breasts and legs, then rub pepper in well. • Wash and finely chop soup vegetables. Peel second onion and dice. • Brown chicken pieces in butter, add prepared soup vegetables and onion and continue to fry. Pour over chicken broth and wine, then cook for 30 minutes until meat is done. The broth should boil down to half its original quantity. • Mix in sour cream and again reduce by half. • Wash and peel or scrape carrots, celery, kohlrabi and leek. Cut in julienne strips and stir into sauce with tarragon

and parsley. Simmer gently for 3 minutes.

Chicken Fricassee with Millet

Wholefood recipe

690 calories per serving
Preparation time: 30 minutes
Cooking time: 1 hour

1 chicken weighing 2¼ lbs.
1 tsp. sea salt
1 small bay leaf
5 white peppercorns
1 vegetable bouillon cube
1 carrot
1¾ cups millet
2¼ cups leek
3 tbs. butter
1 cup cream
2 tbs. freshly chopped parsley
Juice of ½ lemon

Pinch each, salt and freshly ground white pepper

Wash chicken, put in pot with salt, bay leaf, peppercorns and bouillon cube. Cover with water and cook for 1 hour until tender. • Strain broth and measure off 3¼ cups, keeping rest for later use. • Scrape, wash and dice carrot. Add with millet to broth, cover and cook for 30 minutes over low heat until soft. • Clean, halve and wash leeks; cut in strips and cook for 10 minutes in butter. • Take meat off bone, cut in 1½ in. pieces and combine with millet, leek, cream and parsley. Season to taste with lemon juice, salt and pepper.

Chicken Marengo

Classic recipe demanding time in preparation

620 calories per serving
Preparation time: 1 hour

1 chicken weighing 2¾ lbs.
½ tsp. freshly ground white pepper
½ cup olive oil
1¾ cups button mushrooms
Juice of 1 lemon
1 cup chicken broth
6 anchovy fillets
2 cloves garlic
Sprig parsley
2 sprigs thyme
½ bay leaf
1¾ cups tomatoes
12 black olives
2 hard boiled eggs

Wash chicken and giblets. Cut chicken in 8 serving pieces, pat dry and rub well with pepper and a small amount of olive oil. • Clean and wash mushrooms, slice and sprinkle with lemon juice. • Heat chicken broth. Chop anchovies finely. Peel and chop garlic. Wash and dry herbs, tie in bunch with bay leaf. • Brown chicken pieces thoroughly in remaining oil for 10 minutes. Add mushrooms, anchovies, garlic, herbs and hot chicken broth; cover and simmer all together over medium heat for 25 minutes. • Skin and chop tomatoes, removing cores. Add tomato and olives to chicken for final 5 minutes of cooking time. • Peel and finely chop hardboiled eggs. Sprinkle over dish just before serving.

Braised Paprika Chicken

Economical specialty from Hungary

480 calories per serving
Preparation time: 50 minutes

1 chicken weighing 2¾ lbs.
2 medium onions
4 green peppers
3 tbs. clarified butter
6 tbs. chicken broth
½ cup sour cream
1 tbs. mild paprika
1 tsp. salt
Pinch freshly ground white pepper
1 tbs. finely chopped parsley

Wash chicken (and any giblets there may be) thoroughly both inside and out, dry well and divide into 8 serving pieces. • Peel and finely chop onions. Halve peppers, remove stems, ribs and seeds, wash in lukewarm water. Then dry and cut in 1¼ in. wide strips. • Heat clarified butter in a large, heavy bottomed pan and fry onions until transparent, turning continuously. • Add chicken pieces and continue to fry for a few minutes, suntil turning. Add prepared pepper and chicken broth, cover and cook gently over low heat for 30 minutes. • Meanwhile, stir sour cream, paprika, salt and pepper together; add to chicken at the end of 30 minutes. Allow to stand for 5 minutes on hotplate once it is switched off. Sprinkle parsley over chicken before serving. • Boiled rice goes best with this dish.

Chicken Bearnaise

Classic French recipe

760 calories per serving
Preparation time: 40 minutes
Cooking time: 1½ hours

1 chicken weighing 2¾ lbs.
1 dry bread roll
6 oz. boiled ham, minus fat
1 clove garlic
7 oz. sausage meat
2 tbs. chopped chives
4 cups water
1 tsp. salt
Sprig fresh thyme
2 sprigs flat-leaved parsley
1 bay leaf
1 small onion
2 small carrots
1 small piece celery
2 small leeks
1¾ cups savoy cabbage
1 cup string beans

Wash and dry chicken and giblets. • Soak bread roll in cold water. • Dice ham and giblets. Peel and chop garlic, then mix together with ham, giblets, sausage meat, chives and roll, from which water has been squeezed. • Fill chicken with stuffing, fastening opening together with toothpicks. • Bring water to a boil with salt, herbs and bay leaf. Put in chicken and cook, covered, for 1 hour. • Peel and chop onion. Clean or scrape carrots, celery and leeks, then wash and chop them. Cut cabbage in fine strips. Clean and wash beans, then break in pieces. Add prepared vegetables to chicken and cook all together for 30 minutes longer.

Braised Rosemary Chicken

Economical and simple to prepare

430 calories per serving
Preparation time: 1 hour

1 roasting chicken weighing 2¾ lbs.
1 tsp. salt
2 tbs. clarified butter
½ cup hot chicken broth
1 sprig rosemary
1 small cooking apple
1 small floury potato
½ cup dry white wine
Pinch each, salt and freshly ground white pepper

Wash chicken and giblets thoroughly, then dry them. Cut chicken in 8 serving portions and rub well with salt. • Melt clarified butter in heavy bot-tomed pot and brown chicken pieces on all sides. Add chicken stock and rosemary, together with heart and gizzard, cover and simmer on low heat for 30 min-utes. • Meanwhile, chop liver finely. Peel apple. Peel potato under running water, rinse and grate with apple. Add grated ap-ple and potato, liver and white wine to chicken, pouring in a lit-tle more broth if necessary. • Continue to braise chicken for 10 more minutes, seasoning to taste with salt and pepper. • Serve with wide ribbon noodles.

Chicken Drumsticks in a Roasting Bag

Economical and easy to prepare

310 calories per serving
Preparation time: 20 minutes
Cooking time: 35 minutes

4 chicken drumsticks weighing 7 oz. each
1 tsp. salt
1 tbs. mild paprika
2 tbs. clarified butter
2 shallots
1 cup leeks, white part only
¼ cauliflower
2 red peppers
½ cup chicken broth
2 tbs. medium sherry
2 tbs. chopped chives

Wash and dry drumsticks, rub well with salt and pa-prika, then brown thoroughly in clarified butter over low heat. • Preheat oven to 425°F removing wire shelf. • Peel shallots and cut in eighths. Clean and halve leeks, wash these and cut in 1¼ in. pieces. • Divide cau-liflower in florets, wash thor-oughly and leave to drain. • Cut peppers in half, remove stem, ribs and seeds, wash and chop in pieces. • Lift drumsticks out of fat and place in roasting bag with prepared vegetables and chicken broth. Seal bag well, piercing up-per surface several times with a needle. • Lay roasting bag on cold wire shelf, slide onto second rail of oven and cook for 5 min-utes. • Transfer drumsticks and vegetables with cooking juices to a serving dish. • Sprinkle with sherry and chives. • Serve with plain boiled potatoes.

Chicken Pie

Wholefood recipe

930 calories per serving
Preparation time: 1½ hours
Baking time: 25 minutes

1 chicken weighing 2¼ lbs.
4 cups water
1 tsp. sea salt
1¼ cups wholewheat flour
1 tsp. baking powder
1 pinch each, sea salt, curry powder and freshly ground black pepper
¾ cup softened butter
1 egg
1 onion
1 carrot
1 cup button mushrooms
1 tbs. chopped parsley
1 tsp. chopped basil
½ tsp. each, sea salt and freshly ground white pepper
Pinch cayenne pepper
For the pie dish: butter
For the glaze: 1 egg yolk

Wash chicken, cover with salted water and cook for 1 hour. • Mix 1 cup flour with baking powder, curry powder and pepper, then knead to a dough with butter and egg. Put to one side to rest. • Peel and finely chop onion, then fry until transparent in remaining butter. • Scrape carrot, wash and clean it with mushrooms, then chop all finely. Fry for 5 minutes with onion. • Lift chicken out of broth, take meat off bone and cut in 1 in. pieces. Measure out 1 cup stock, putting rest aside to use elsewhere. • Mix remaining flour to a thin paste with broth and add to vegetables, allowing all to simmer for 5 minutes longer. Add meat, herbs and spices. • Preheat oven to 400°F. Grease pie dish and pour in meat filling. • Roll pastry out somewhat bigger than dish, lay on filling and press edges down firmly on to dish. Prick lid well and brush with egg yolk. • Bake for 25 minutes until brown.

Circassian Chicken

A specialty from Russia which requires a certain amount of time

750 calories per serving
Preparation time: 40 minutes
Cooking time: 1½ hours

1 chicken weighing 2¾ lbs.
1 tsp. salt
Soup vegetables
1 medium and 1 small onion
1 bay leaf
1 clove
½ dry bread roll
¾ cup shelled walnuts
2 tsp. oil
1 tsp. salt
1 tbs. chopped parsley
2 tbs. sour cream

W ash chicken and giblets, add salt, cover with boiling water and bring back to a boil.

Remove any scum that forms during first 30 minutes. • Poach chicken for 30 minutes on such a low heat that cooking liquid only just moves. • Wash, clean and chop soup vegetables roughly. Peel and quarter medium onion, then spike bay leaf to one quarter with clove. • After 30 minutes add prepared vegetables to chicken and continue to simmer for 1 hour longer until chicken is done. • Soak roll in cold water. Peel small onion and chop finely. Grind two-thirds of nuts and coarsely chop the rest. Heat oil and fry onion until golden brown, then add ground nuts and fry briefly. Squeeze water from roll, crumble it and mix to a smooth paste with fried onion and nuts, salt, parsley, chopped nuts and sour cream. • Remove chicken from bouillon, take meat off the bone and cut in pieces, then keep warm. • Strain bouillon and reduce

slightly by boiling uncovered. • Stir ¾ cup bouillon stock into nut mixture, then add meat to sauce. • Serve with fluffy boiled rice.

Turkey Fricassee

Rather more expensive but quick

310 calories per serving
Preparation time: 25 minutes

2¼ lbs. turkey steak
1 tbs. flour
1 onion
2 tbs. coconut oil
⅓ cup chicken bouillon
Bunch mixed herbs (chervil, tarragon, parsley)
1 tsp. curry powder
¾ cup sour cream
1 tbs. small capers
2 pinches each, salt and freshly ground white pepper

W ash and pat dry meat, then cut in fine strips and coat in flour. • Peel onion and chop finely. • Heat oil in large pan. Brown meat quickly on high heat, turning frequently. Add onion and continue to fry, then gradually add bouillon. Simmer together for 5 minutes. • Wash and dry herbs before chopping finely. • Stir curry powder into sour cream and add to chicken mixture with capers and herbs. Season with salt and pepper. • Serve with buttered noodles and a mixed salad.

Creamed Chicken

Requires time for preparation

800 calories per serving
Preparation time: 30 minutes
Cooking time: 1½ hours

1 chicken weighing 2¾ lbs.
6 cups water
2 tsp. salt
1 large carrot
2 onions
2 leeks
⅛ celery
1 cup cream
1 tbs. medium sherry
1–2 pinches salt
1–2 tsp. curry powder
1 tsp. lemon juice
4 slices white bread weighing 2 oz. each
4 tbs. butter

Wash chicken and giblets. Bring water and salt to a boil, then add chicken. Keep skimming off any scum that forms during first 20 minutes. • Scrape and rinse carrot, cut in pieces. Peel onions and cut in 8. Wash leeks and celery before chopping roughly. Add prepared vegetables to chicken and reduce heat until stock barely simmers. Poach chicken gently, uncovered, for 1 hour longer. • Lift chicken from broth, remove skin, take meat off the bone and cut in small, even pieces. • Pour cream over meat and reduce slightly. Season sauce to taste with sherry, salt, curry powder and lemon juice, thinning with a few tablespoons of chicken broth if necessary. • Fry slices of bread in foaming butter until brown on both sides, divide between 4 plates and spoon over chicken fricassee. • Serve immediately.

Chicken a la King

Quick wholefood recipe

310 calories per serving
Preparation time: 35 minutes

1¾ cups button mushrooms
1¼ lbs. chicken breast fillets
1 red pepper
2 tbs. butter
1 cup cream
2 tbs. wholewheat flour
½ cup chicken broth
1 tsp. seasoning salt
Pinch freshly ground black pepper
Juice of 1 lemon
1 tbs. chopped parsley

Wash, clean and finely slice mushrooms. • Wash chicken, remove any skin or bones and cut in ½ in. wide strips. • Halve pepper, remove stalk, ribs and seeds, then blanch 5 minutes in boiling salted water, drain and dice. • Melt butter. Fry mushrooms and chicken strips for 5 minutes, turning frequently. • Whisk cream with flour and broth, before adding to chicken. Add diced pepper. Simmer gently for 5 minutes, adding a little more broth if necessary to form a creamy sauce. • Remove pan from heat, season to taste with seasoning salt, pepper and lemon juice, then sprinkle with parsley.

Basque Chicken

Specialty from Spain, requiring a certain amount of time

690 calories per serving
Preparation time: 1 hour

1 chicken weighing 2¼ lbs.
3½ cups tomatoes
2 green peppers
2 onions
3 cloves garlic
5 tbs. olive oil
½ cup hot chicken bouillon
1½ tsp. salt
2 pinches freshly ground black pepper
1¼ cups long grain rice
1 tbs. mild paprika

Wash and dry chicken and giblets. Cut chicken in 8 pieces. • Skin and quarter tomatoes, removing core. • Halve and clean peppers, then wash and dry them before cutting in strips. • Peel onions and garlic and chop finely. • Heat 3 tbs. oil. Brown chicken pieces thoroughly. Add onion and garlic and continue to fry, turning frequently, until soft. • Add tomato, green pepper, bouillon, 1 tsp. salt and pepper, then cover and simmer for 30 minutes. • Wash and drain rice well before frying in remaining oil. Pour in twice as much water as there is rice, add ½ tsp. salt, cover and cook over low heat for 20 minutes or until rice is done. Stir in paprika, put into serving dish and arrange chicken and vegetables on top.

Chicken in Peanut Sauce

Economical wholefood recipe

550 calories per serving
Preparation time: 50 minutes

1 chicken weighing 2¼ lbs.
1 tsp. sea salt
½ tsp. freshly ground white pepper
1 tbs. butter
1 cup carrots
1 cup shelled peanuts
2 tbs. wholewheat flour
½ tsp. ground tumeric
¾ cup hot water
2 tbs. chopped parsley

Cut chicken into 4 pieces, wash and dry them before rubbing with salt and pepper. • Melt butter in skillet. Brown chicken thoroughly before covering and cooking very gently for 40 minutes, turning once. • Wash and peel carrots, then dice very finely. • Coarsely grind peanuts and sprinkle with flour over chicken in skillet. Turn pieces in this mixture, fry briefly again, then add diced carrot, turmeric and water. Continue to simmer for about 10 minutes more until sauce thickens. • Taste sauce for seasoning. Sprinkle with parsley. • Serve with potato croquettes.

Poached Chicken

Requires a certain amount of time

480 calories per serving
Preparation time: 30 minutes
Cooking time: 1½ hours

2 chickens weighing 1¾ lbs. each
2 tsp. salt
Soup vegetables
4 small onions
1 bay leaf
1 clove
4 medium carrots
4 leeks
4 small potatoes
1 sprig each, parsley, celery top and thyme

Wash chickens and giblets, then put into large pot with salt. • Wash and clean soup vegetables. Peel 1 onion, spike bay leaf on it with clove, then add all prepared vegetables to pot. Pour on sufficient boiling water to cover chickens. Bring back to boil, then turn down heat so that liquid barely simmers and continue to cook in this way for 1 hour. • Skim off any scum that forms during first 30 minutes of cooking time. • Peel remaining onions. Peel and wash carrots, then cut in 4 lengthwise. Halve white part of leeks lengthwise, wash thoroughly and halve again lengthwise. Peel, wash and halve potatoes. • Rinse herbs in warm water, dry and tie in bouquet garni. After 1 hour add prepared vegetables and herbs to pot, cover and continue to poach for 30 minutes longer. • Remove chickens from bouillon, cut in serving pieces and arrange on warmed dish with vegetables. • Strain bouillon and serve as clear soup beforehand.

Bolivian Chicken

An easy-to-prepare specialty

740 calories per serving
Preparation time: 40 minutes
Cooking time: 1 hour

1 chicken weighing 3¼ lbs.
2 cloves garlic
3 large onions
¼ cup olive oil
1½ cups hot meat bouillon
1 tsp. salt
2 pinches freshly ground black pepper
1 tsp. hot paprika
1¾ cups tomatoes
1 red pepper
½ tsp. dried oregano
1 tsp. caraway seeds
5 tbs. fresh breadcrumbs
2 hard boiled eggs
20 green olives

Wash chicken and giblets, then cut chicken in 8 pieces. Peel and finely chop garlic. • Peel onions and cut in rings, then cook two-thirds in oil until transparent. Add chicken pieces and brown thoroughly. • Pour in half hot bouillon, stir in salt, pepper and paprika. Cover and simmer together for 40 minutes. • Peel and chop tomatoes. Halve and clean red pepper, then wash and dry it before cutting in dice. • Combine prepared tomato and red pepper with remaining bouillon, oregano, caraway seeds, remaining onion rings and garlic. Cover and simmer gently for 20 minutes. At the end of this time stir in breadcrumbs. • Serve chicken pieces together with vegetables and sauce, garnished with sliced eggs and olives.

Chicken in Apricot Sauce

Rumanian specialty which is easy to prepare

550 calories per serving
Preparation time: 40 minutes
Cooking time: 30 minutes

1 oven-ready chicken weighing 2¾ lbs.
1 large onion
2¼ cups apricots
6 tbs. corn oil
2 tbs. flour
1¼ cups hot water
2 tsp. brown sugar
1 tsp. salt
3 pinches freshly ground white pepper

Peel and finely chop onion. Wash apricots in warm water, dry and halve them, removing stones. • Wash chicken and giblets, pat dry and cut chicken in 8 pieces. • Heat oil in large, heavy bottomed skillet. Brown chicken pieces thoroughly over medium heat, then remove from skillet. • Pour off all but 1 tbs. oil. Sprinkle in flour, and add sufficient water, stirring constantly, to make a thick sauce. • Stir in chopped onion and simmer for a few minutes over low heat. Then stir in apricot halves. Add sugar, salt and pepper, then chicken pieces. • Cover skillet and continue to simmer over low heat for 30 minutes longer. • Serve with fluffy boiled rice or mashed potato and a salad.

Chicken with Eggplants

Sicilian specialty

670 calories per serving
Preparation time: 1 hour

1 frying chicken weighing 2¾ lbs.	
3 medium eggplants, approx. 1¼ lbs. total	
1 tsp. salt	
1 clove garlic	
2 oz. slices of bacon	
1¼ cup ripe tomatoes	
6 tbs. olive oil	
⅓ cup dry white wine	
½ tsp. oregano	
2 pinches salt	
1 pinch freshly ground white pepper	
1 bunch parsley	

Wash and dice eggplants (unpeeled), sprinkle with salt and put aside to drain for 30 minutes. • Chop garlic and dice bacon. • Cut a cross in skin of tomatoes, immerse in boiling water, skin and chop. • Cut chicken in 8 pieces. Wash and dry both chicken and giblets. • Heat 3 tbs. oil in large, heavy bottomed skillet with lid. Brown chicken pieces thoroughly with diced bacon and chopped garlic. • Add wine and allow it to boil away. • Add tomatoes, oregano, salt and pepper, cover and cook on low heat for 25 minutes. • Rinse diced eggplants and drain well. Fry in remaining oil over high heat for 7 minutes, turning constantly. Add to chicken mixture. • Wash and dry parsley before chopping finely and sprinkle it over dish just before serving.

Braised Herbed Chicken

Economical and easy to prepare

500 calories per serving
Preparation time: 45 minutes
Cooking time: 30 minutes

1 chicken weighing 2¾ lbs.	
3 tbs. butter	
½ tsp. salt	
2 pinches freshly ground black pepper	
Juice of ½ lemon	
⅓ cup dry white wine	
3 tbs. chicken bouillon	
5 shallots	
Bunch parsley	
5 sprigs basil	
1 organically grown lemon	

Wash and dry chicken and giblets. Cut chicken in 8 pieces and brown thoroughly in butter over low heat. Season with salt and pepper, sprinkle with lemon juice and add half the wine. • Cover and simmer chicken and giblets for 30 minutes, turning several times and adding bouillon as necessary. • Peel shallots and chop finely with washed parsley and basil leaves. Wash lemon in warm water, dry and cut in 8 segments. Remove chicken from skillet and keep warm. • Finely chop liver, rejecting rest of giblets. • Cook shallots in braising juices, without browning. • Add chopped liver and remaining wine, then reduce to a thick sauce. • Reheat chicken in sauce, sprinkle with chopped herbs and serve garnished with lemon segments.

Chicken and Fennel Risotto

Easy to prepare

2¼ lbs. chicken breast
1 tsp. salt
Pinch freshly ground white pepper
½ tsp. dried tarragon
3 cups fennel
2 onions
1 large clove garlic
6 tbs. olive oil
1¼ cups round grain rice
1½ cups chicken bouillon
¾ cup dry white wine
½ tsp. salt
1 cup freshly grated Parmesan cheese

Wash and pat dry chicken breasts, then cut in half and rub well with salt, pepper and tarragon. • Cut off some green leaves from fennel, wash and put aside. Trim fennel stalks, quarter heads and wash. • Peel and dice onions and garlic. • Heat oil and brown chicken breasts well on both sides. Add fennel, onion and garlic and fry briefly together. • Wash rice in sieve, drain well and dry in a clean cloth. Add to skillet with chicken and saute, stirring constantly, for a few minutes. Pour chicken bouillon and white wine over mixture, season with salt, cover and cook for 20 minutes. • Chop fennel leaves finely and scatter over risotto with Parmesan cheese.

Tip: The final touch can be given to this risotto with the addition of ¼ cup toasted pine kernels.

Chicken with Olives

Easy to prepare

500 calories per serving
Preparation time: 25 minutes
Cooking time: 30 minutes

1 chicken weighing 2¾ lbs.
1 sprig rosemary
2 cloves garlic
2 ripe beefsteak tomatoes
16 black or green olives
¼ cup olive oil
1 tsp. salt
Pinch freshly ground white pepper
3 tbs. chicken bouillon
2 sprigs basil

Cut chicken in 8 pieces; wash and pat dry, together with giblets. • Wash and dry rosemary, removing leaves from stalk. Peel garlic and chop finely with rosemary. • Slit round end of tomatoes crosswise, immerse in boiling water, remove skin and core, then cut in pieces. Stone olives. • Heat oil in large, heavy bottomed skillet with lid. Brown chicken pieces and giblets thoroughly over medium heat, sprinkle on garlic and rosemary mixture and continue to fry briefly. Season with salt and pepper, cover skillet and braise gently for 15 minutes on low heat. • Add tomato pieces, olives and bouillon, simmer for 15 minutes longer, adding more bouillon if necessary. • Wash, dry and chop basil leaves. Scatter over chicken before serving. • Fried polenta or crusty French bread are good with this dish.

Chicken Souffle

Slightly more difficult

380 calories per serving
Preparation time: 20 minutes
Cooking time: 1 hour

| 1¼ lbs chicken breasts (with bone) |
| 1 small bay leaf |
| ½ tsp. white peppercorns |
| 1 tsp. salt |
| 2 sprigs parsley |
| ½ tsp. tarragon |
| ⅓ cup water |
| 4 shallots |
| 2 tbs. butter |
| 2 tbs. flour |
| 6 tbs. cream |
| ¼ cup dry white wine |
| 2 pinches white pepper |
| 4 eggs |
| 1 tbs. grated Parmesan cheese |
| Butter for greasing souffle dishes |

Wash chicken breasts, put into boiling water, together with bay leaf, peppercorns, salt, parsley and tarragon. Cover and simmer gently for 30 minutes. • Take meat off bone and cut in thin slivers. Strain bouillon. • Peel and dice shallots, then fry until transparent in butter. Sprinkle in flour, continuing to fry until light brown. Add bouillon gradually, then cream and white wine. Stir well while bringing to a boil. Season to taste with salt and pepper. • Preheat oven to 400°F. Butter souffle dishes well. • Separate eggs. Stir egg yolks, cheese and chicken into sauce. • Beat egg whites until very stiff and fold carefully into mixture. Spoon quickly into prepared dishes and bake in center of oven for 30 minutes. Serve immediately.

Drumsticks with Mushrooms

Easy to prepare

520 calories per serving
Preparation time: 40 minutes
Cooking time: 30 minutes

| 8 chicken drumsticks |
| ¼ cup flour |
| 1 onion |
| 1 clove garlic |
| 1 tbs. butter |
| ¼ cup olive oil |
| 1 tbs. tomato paste |
| ⅓ cup dry red wine |
| 1 tsp. salt |
| 2 pinches white pepper |
| Pinch each marjoram and thyme |
| Bunch parsley |
| 1½ cups button mushrooms |
| Juice of ½ lemon |
| 1 tbs. wine vinegar |

Wash drumsticks and coat with flour. • Peel and chop onion and garlic. • Heat butter with 1 tbs. oil. Brown drumsticks, adding onion and garlic and frying until tender. • Combine tomato paste with red wine, salt, pepper, marjoram and thyme, add to chicken and cook gently for 30 minutes. • Wash and finely chop parsley. Clean and slice mushrooms, then sprinkle with lemon juice. • Heat remaining oil in separate skillet. Fry half of parsley and all mushrooms in it, cooking until all juices have evaporated. • Add mushroom mixture to chicken, sprinkle with vinegar and remaining parsley before serving.

Szechuan Chicken

Specialty from China

480 calories per serving
Preparation time: 1 hour

1 chicken weighing 2¼ lbs.
3 tbs. light soy sauce
2 tsp. cornstarch
3 carrots
4 scallions or green onions
1 hot red chili (fresh)
¼ cup sesame oil

Wash and pat dry chicken, then split in half and bone. • Cut meat in thin, 2 in. long strips. Place strips in bowl and sprinkle with soy sauce and cornstarch. Thoroughly combine and cover bowl and marinate for 30 minutes. • Peel carrots under running water. Trim, wash and dry scallions or green onions.

Shred both finely. Wash chili in warm water, dry, remove stalk and seeds before cutting in fine rings. • Heat 2 tbs. oil in wok or large skillet. Fry chicken strips for 5 minutes, turning continuously, then remove from skillet. • Heat remaining oil in wok or skillet and fry vegetables for 6 minutes, again stirring constantly. Add meat and stir-fry together for 2 minutes longer. • Serve with fluffy boiled rice and soy sauce.

Chicken Breast with Cheese Sauce

Quick and easy

740 calories per serving
Preparation time: 30 minutes

1¼ lbs. chicken breast
4 pinches each, salt and freshly ground white pepper
1 tbs. flour
1 egg
½ cup blanched almonds, chopped
3 tbs. clarified butter
3 tbs. dry white wine
1¼ cup cream
½ cup Gorgonzola cheese
Pinch freshly grated nutmeg
Pinch sugar

Wash and dry chicken breast, then rub salt and pepper into both sides. Coat breast first in flour, then in lightly beaten egg and finally in chopped almonds. Press coating firmly onto chicken. • Heat clarified butter in skillet. Fry chicken breast for about 4 minutes on each side over medium heat. Remove from skillet and keep warm. • Deglaze skillet with wine and cream, stirring as sauce comes to a boil. Cut rind off Gorgonzola, mash with a fork and add to sauce, stirring as it melts. Season sauce with nutmeg, sugar and additional salt and white pepper if required. • Arrange chicken on dish with cheese sauce and serve hot. • Ribbon noodles with buttered broccoli or a green salad go well with this dish.

Champagne Fricassee

More expensive but quick to prepare

500 calories per serving
Preparation time: 35 minutes

1¼ lb. chicken breast
Large sprig tarragon
2 pinches white pepper
Juice of ½ lemon
2 shallots
7 oz. shrimp, peeled
¼ cup butter
1 cup light crea
1 egg yolk
1 small bottle (3 oz.) dry champagne
1 tsp. salt
Pinch cayenne pepper

Rinse chicken breasts in warm water and pat dry. Rinse and dry tarragon before chopping leaves finely. Rub pepper into chicken breasts, sprinkle with chopped tarragon and lemon juice, cover and marinate for 10 minutes. • Peel and chop shallots. • Rinse and pat dry shrimp, removing black vein if necessary. • Take chicken out of marinade and dry thoroughly. Put marinade aside. Cut chicken in strips, ½ in. wide. • Heat butter in large heavy bottomed skillet until foamy, then fry chicken strips for 4 minutes, turning frequently so that they brown evenly. Add shallots and fry for 1 minute more. • Add shrimp and continue to fry, turning constantly, for another minute. • Beat cream with egg yolk, stir into fricassee and heat through gently, without allowing mixture to boil. Pour in champagne and reheat, again not allowing fricassee to boil. • Season well with salt, cayenne pepper and marinade. • Serve with green ribbon noodles or potato croquettes and buttered petits pois.

Braised Partridge with Lentils

**Preparation requiring time
Also rather expensive**

Soaking time: 30 minutes
Preparation time: 50 minutes
Cooking time: 1½ hours

2 partridges weighing 1 lb. 2 oz. each
1¼ cups lentils
1 leek, white part only
¾ cups carrots
¾ cups bacon
2 cloves
1 bay leaf
1 tsp. salt
2 pinches freshly ground white pepper
3 small onions weighing 2 oz. each
¼ cup dry white wine
¾ cup meat bouillon
1 cup sour cream

Put lentils into large bowl of water and pick over, tipping out floating dirt and rejects. Pour lentils into sieve, rinse well and drain thoroughly. Then put into pot, cover with water and leave to soak for 30 minutes. • Halve leek lengthwise, wash and dry, then cut in julienne strips. Peel carrots under running water, dry and cut in rings. Cut rind off bacon. • Add prepared leek and carrots together with bacon rind to lentils and water, cover and simmer gently for 1½ hours. Add cloves and bay leaf after first 30 minutes. • Wash partridges inside and out, then dry and rub inside with salt, outside with pepper. Peel onions and cut in 8 pieces. Cut bacon in strips. • Fry bacon strips in large skillet until crisp and golden, then remove from skillet. • Preheat oven to 400°F. • Brown partridges all over in bacon fat. Remove from skillet and put side by side into casserole, sprinkle with bacon fat and surround with onion pieces. • Roast for 30 minutes in center of oven. • After 30 minutes, reduce temperature to 325°F. Pour wine and bouillon over partridges, cover and continue to cook for 45 minutes more. • Once all cooking liquid has been absorbed by lentils, remove bay leaf, cloves and bacon rind. Season lentils with salt and pepper, then arrange in deep serving dish and keep warm. • Halve partridges and arrange on top of lentils. • Combine cooking juices from game with sour cream in small pan and reduce until smooth and creamy, stirring frequently. Pour sauce over partridges. • Reheat bacon strips briefly in skillet, then scatter over partridges. • Serve with mashed potatoes and onion rings browned in butter.

Duck Flambe

Somewhat expensive

Total preparation time: 50 minutes

2 boned duck breasts, weighing 10 oz. each
1½ cups plums
2 pinches each, salt and freshly ground white pepper
1 tbs. butter
2 tbs.brandy
1 cup sour cream
1 cup cream
Pinch ground cinnamon
Pinch cayenne pepper

Wash and pat dry duck breasts. Remove skin and cut in fine strips. • Wash, dry, halve and stone plums. • Put strips of skin into skillet without fat, cover and fry until crisp and brown. Take out of skillet. •

Using fat suntil in skillet, fry duck breasts for 3 minutes on each side, then season with salt and pepper and remove from skillet. Wrap in aluminium foil to keep warm. • Pour away duck fat. Heat butter in skillet and fry plums until juicy without losing their shape. • Heat duck and juices gently with plums. • Add brandy and heat, then set alight. After 3 seconds, put lid on skillet. • Keep duck and plums warm on serving dish. Combine cooking juices with sour cream, cream, cinnamon and cayenne pepper, seasoning to taste with salt and pepper. • Carve duck breasts in thin diagonal slices, and scatter with crispy skin. Serve sauce separately. • Good accompanied by potato fritters and a green salad.

Guinea Fowl a la Normande

Specialty from France

1100 calories per serving
Preparation time: 50 minutes
Cooking time: 55 minutes

2 guinea fowl weighing 1¾ lbs. each
1 tsp. salt
Pinch white pepper
3 tbs. oil
¼ cup shelled walnuts
½ tsp. thyme
¾ cup cider
1 cup sour cream
6 tbs. Calvados
2 thin slices of bacon
2¼ cups firm, tart apples
2 tbs. butter
1 tsp. sugar

Preheat oven to 400°F. • Wash and dry guinea fowl, then rub well with salt and pepper. Brown quickly in oil in heavy bottomed skillet, remove from skillet and pour off all except 1 tbs. of fat. • Put walnuts and thyme into skillet and fry, stirring, for 1 minute beffore slowly adding cider, sour cream and Calvados. Lay guinea fowl on backs in sauce, covering breasts with 1 slice bacon each. Cover and cook in oven for 45 minutes. • Peel, core and slice apples. Heat butter, fry apple slices gently for 10 minutes, then sprinkle with sugar. • Brown guinea fowl on wire rack in oven for 10 minutes, and reduce sauce. • Carve guinea fowl and serve with sauce, garnished with apple slices.

Duck with Olives

Easy to prepare, though requires time

1100 calories per serving
Preparation time: 45 minutes
Cooking time: 1 hour

1 duckling weighing 3¼ lbs.	
1 onion	
1 clove garlic	
1 bunch each, parsley and basil	
2 tbs. small capers	
3 tbs. olive oil	
1 tsp. salt	
2 pinches freshly ground black pepper	
⅓ cup dry white wine	
⅓ cup chicken bouillon	
2 duck livers	
¼ cup green olives	

Wash duck, dry thoroughly and cut in 8 pieces. • Peel onion and garlic. Wash and dry herbs. Finely chop onion, garlic, capers and herbs. • Heat oil in heavy bottomed skillet. Brown duck pieces on all sides, reduce heat and add chopped onion and seasonings. Continue to fry gently for 10 more minutes, then season with salt and pepper. • Pour in wine and allow to evaporate slowly over low heat, stirring continuously. Then add bouillon, cover skillet and simmer duck gently for about 1 hour. • Wash and dry livers, remove any fat or membrane, then chop finely. Stone olives and add with chopped liver to duck shortly before end of cooking time. Simmer briefly, stirring well. • Serve with white bread and tomato salad.

Duck with Tomato

Requires time to prepare

1000 calories per serving
Marinating time: 3 hours
Preparation time: 40 minutes
Cooking time: 1 hour

1 duckling weighing 3¼ lbs.	
2 sprigs rosemary	
6 black peppercorns	
⅓ cup dry white wine	
⅓ cup wine vinegar	
1 large onion	
2½ cups ripe tomatoes	
¼ cup olive oil	
Pinch powdered saffron	
1 tsp. salt	
½ tsp. black pepper	
5 tbs. chicken bouillon	

Cut duck in 8 pieces, wash and dry them, then put in bowl. • Add rosemary sprigs, peppercorns, wine and vinegar. • Marinate duck for 3 hours in mixture, turning occasionally. • Peel onion and slice in thin rings. Cut shallow cross in tomato skins, immerse in boiling water, remove skin and core before coarsely chopping. • Heat oil in heavy bottomed skillet and fry onion until golden brown. Add tomatoes and saffron, season with salt and pepper, then cover and simmer for 15 minutes. • Take duck pieces out of marinade and drain before putting into tomato sauce with chicken bouillon. Cover again and simmer gently over low heat for 1 hour, adding more bouillon if necessary. • Adjust seasoning to taste. • Serve with rice and green salad.

Duck in Pineapple Sauce

Easy to prepare

680 calories per serving
Preparation time: 25 minutes
Cooking time: 1 hour

1 duckling weighing 3¼ lbs.
1 tbs. corn oil
⅓ cup pineapple juice
¾ cup dry red wine
½ tsp. salt
2 pinches freshly ground white pepper
Juice of 1 lemon
1 tbs. cornstarch
Juice and grated peel of 1 organically grown orange
1¾ cup fresh pineapple
1 tbs. pineapple jam

Preheat oven to 400°F. • Wash duck and pat dry before cutting in 6 pieces. Brush with oil, lay in casserole and roast in oven for 20 minutes. • Combine pineapple juice with red wine, salt, pepper and lemon juice, pour over duck and baste with mixture repeatedly during remaining 40 minutes cooking time. • Mix cornstarch with orange juice. • Quarter and peel pineapple, remove hard core and cut in wedges. • After 1 hour remove duck from oven and place pieces in warm serving dish. Keep warm in switched-off oven. • Skim fat off roasting juices, then strain juices. Combine with cornstarch mixture, bring to a boil and stir in grated orange peel with additional water if necessary. Add pineapple pieces and jam to sauce, season well with salt and white pepper, then pour over duck. • Serve with glazed yams (sweet potatoes).

Wild Duck in Beaujolais Sauce

Specialty from France, rather more expensive

760 calories per serving
Preparation time: 1 hour
Cooking time: 1 hour

2 young wild ducks, weighing 3¼ lbs. each
3¼ cups celery root
1¼ cup potatoes
1 tsp. salt
Pinch white pepper
2 tbs. butter
⅓ cup cream
2 tsp. lemon juice
2-3 stalks parsley, chopped
2 pinches black pepper
1 bunch marjoram
2 shallots
¾ cup Beaujolais
¼ cup ice cold butter

Peel, wash and dice celery root and potatoes. Cover with water and boil for 20 minutes, then purée in food processor together with ½ tsp. salt, pepper, butter and cream. Season with lemon juice, sprinkle with parsley and keep warm. • Preheat oven to 425°F. • Wash ducks inside and out, pat dry and rub well with remaining salt and pepper. • Wash marjoram and put half in each cavity. Roast ducks in oven for 20 minutes. • Remove breasts from ducks, carve in thin slices and keep warm. Pour off cooking juices. • Return remainder of ducks to oven and roast for 40 minutes more at 400°F. • Finely chop shallots, combine with wine and cooking juices in saucepan and reduce by about one half. • Season sauce with salt and pepper and stir in butter cut in small pieces. • Pour half the sauce over sliced duck breast. Carve rest of meat and serve all with remaining sauce, accompanied by celery root.

Goulash with a Difference

Easy to prepare

360 calories per serving
Total preparation time: 45 minutes

1 lb. 2 oz. turkey breast
2 onions
1 tart apple
1¾ cup celery
2 tbs. clarified butter
1 tsp. mild paprika
1 tsp. curry powder
Pinch ground coriander
¾ cup hot meat bouillon
1 tbs. cornstarch
⅓ cup pouring cream
1 mandarin
½ tsp. salt
¼ cup coarsely chopped walnuts

Wash and dry turkey breast, then cut in 1 in. cubes.

Peel onions and cut in eighths. Wash, dry, peel and quarter apple, removing core and cutting quarters in ¼ in. slices. Remove tough strings from celery, trim both ends before washing and drying, then slicing thinly. • Heat clarified butter in large, heavy bottomed skillet. Brown cubed turkey, then reduce heat, add onion and fry for 2 minutes longer. Stir in paprika, curry and coriander, then gradually pour on hot bouillon. Add prepared apple and celery, cover goulash and simmer over low heat for 15 minutes. • Combine cornstarch and cream, stir into sauce and bring to boil again. • Peel mandarin, remove pits and skin from segments. Stir into goulash, together with salt. Scatter chopped nuts over finished dish.

Duck Goulash

Rather more expensive

900 calories per serving
Preparation time: 40 minutes
Cooking time: 1 hour

1 duckling weighing 3¾ lbs.
1 tsp. salt
½ tsp. black pepper
1 tsp. dried marjoram
6 tbs. olive oil
2 onions
1 tsp. mild paprika
½ tsp. dried tarragon
¾ cup dry red wine
⅓ cup chicken bouillon
¼ cup button mushrooms
16 black olives
⅓ cup cream

Wash and dry duck, cut in 12 pieces and rub well with salt, pepper and marjoram. • Heat oil in heavy bottomed skillet and brown pieces over high heat, then remove from skillet. • Peel and finely chop onions. Fry briefly with tomato paste in remaining oil. Add paprika, tarragon, red wine and chicken bouillon; bring mixture to a boil. • Put duck pieces into sauce, cover and braise gently for 1 hour. • Clean mushrooms, cutting bigger ones in two. Add with olives to duck after 30 minutes. • Take duck pieces out of skillet. Reduce cooking sauce by about one half, stirring constantly, then mix in cream. Season well. • Reheat duck pieces in sauce, and serve with millet dumplings or potato croquettes.

Turkey Wings with Peaches

Economical wholefood recipe

570 calories per serving
Preparation time: 30 minutes
Cooking time: 1 hour

1½ lbs. turkey wings
1 small bay leaf
Small quantity soup vegetables
3 white peppercorns
4 pinches sea salt
1 cup soya or millet ribbon noodles
2 qts. water
1 tsp. salt
3 cups ripe peaches
¼ cup butter
½ tsp. freshly ground white pepper
1 tbs. fresh dill
1 tbs. chopped chives

Wash and dry turkey wings, put in saucepan with bay leaf, soup vegetables, peppercorns and 2 pinches salt; cover with water before putting lid on pan and simmering gently for 1 hour until tender. • Cook noodles in boiling salted water for about 10 minutes, then tip into sieve to drain. • Immerse peaches briefly in boiling water before skinning them, cutting in half and removing stones. Slice neatly. • Heat butter in skillet and fry peach slices for 5 minutes, turning frequently. • Remove turkey wings from cooking liquid and cool. Keep bouillon for soup. • Take meat off bone, cut in pieces before sprinkling with remaining salt and pepper. • Combine noodles, peach slices and meat, heat through gently and serve sprinkled with chopped herbs.

Turkey Ragout

Easy to prepare

400 calories per serving
Preparation time: 45 minutes
Cooking time: 15 minutes

1½ lbs. turkey breast
1 large onion
2 cloves garlic
2 oz. bacon
1 large carrot
1 stick celery
2 tbs. olive oil
1 heaping tsp. flour
⅓ cup chicken bouillon
¾ cup dry red wine
½ tsp. salt
½ tsp. freshly ground black pepper
Pinch each, dried marjoram and thyme
½ bay leaf

Peel onion and garlic, chop with bacon. Peel, wash and dice carrot. Trim, wash and slice celery. Chop all vegetables very finely. • Wash, dry and cube meat. • Heat oil in skillet with lid. Fry onion, garlic and bacon until brown and cooked through. Add carrot and celery and continue to fry briefly, stirring well. Next add cubed meat and brown thoroughly. Sprinkle flour over mixture and stir well, then pour in chicken bouillon gradually and bring to a boil. Add wine and continue to boil, uncovered and stirring frequently, until sauce is reduced by half. • Season ragout with salt, pepper, thyme, marjoram and bay leaf, then cover again and simmer over low heat for 15 minutes longer. • Serve accompanied by wholewheat noodles, mashed potato or millet risotto.

Turkey Drumsticks with Tomato

Requires time for preparation

500 calories per serving
Marinating time: 2 hours
Preparation time: 30 minutes
Cooking time: 1¼ hours

2 turkey drumsticks weighing 1¼ lbs. each	
2 cloves garlic	
Sprig rosemary	
1 tsp. salt	
Pinch white pepper	
3 tbs. wine vinegar	
5 anchovy fillets	
1 can peeled tomatoes (14 oz.)	
3 tbs. olive oil	
1 tbs. capers	
2 egg yolks	
Juice of ½ lemon	
1 tbs. butter	

Wash and dry turkey drumsticks. Peel garlic. Wash, dry and destalk rosemary, then finely chop with garlic. • Rub drumsticks with salt, pepper and rosemary and garlic mix, pour over vinegar, cover and put aside to marinate for 2 hours. Turn several times while marinating. • Finely chop anchovies. Drain tomatoes, chop roughly. • Heat oil and brown turkey thoroughly on all sides, then add anchovies. Stir in tomatoes and capers and simmer all together for 1¼ hours, adding some tomato juice if necessary. • Take meat off bone, cut in 1½ in. pieces and reheat in sauce. • Beat egg yolks with lemon juice and stir into sauce with butter.

Turkey Steaks with Coriander

Easy to prepare and economical

260 calories per serving
Total preparation time: 40 minutes

4 turkey steaks weighing 6 oz. each	
1¼ cup shallots	
1 clove garlic	
¼ cup oil	
½ tbs. crushed coriander	
4 pinches salt	
4 pinches freshly ground white pepper	
1 can peeled tomatoes (14 oz.)	
½ chicken bouillon cube	
½ tsp. sugar	
2 pinches cayenne pepper	
Small bunch parsley	

Peel shallots and garlic. Wash and dry steaks. • Heat oil in heavy bottomed skillet and toss coriander in it quickly. Season steaks with salt and pepper, before browning over high heat for 1 minute on each side. Remove from skillet. • Sauté shallots in remaining oil, adding crushed garlic and tomato juice. • Roughly chop tomatoes and put into sauce, then season with crumbled bouillon cube, sugar and cayenne pepper. Reduce slightly, stirring constantly. • Put steaks into sauce, together with any juice that has collected. Cover skillet and warm over low heat for 5 minutes. • Wash, dry and chop parsley, then sprinkle over dish. • Serve with noodles.

Baked and Fried Poultry

Viennese Fried Chicken

Well-known recipe that is easily prepared

475 calories per serving
Total preparation time: 45 minutes

2 chickens weighing 1½ lbs. each
1 tsp. salt
2 eggs
3 tbs. milk
¼ cup flour
⅔ cup fresh breadcrumbs
¾ cup lard
Bunch parsley
1 organically grown lemon

Cut each chicken in 8 portions, then wash and dry them. Rub well with salt. • Beat eggs with milk in flat dish, putting flour and breadcrumbs in two other dishes. • Coat chicken pieces first in flour, shaking off any excess. Next dip in egg mixture, and finally coat with breadcrumbs, pressing crumbs on well. • Heat lard and fry crumbed chicken pieces a few at a time for about 7 minutes, turning to brown evenly. Drain on paper towel. • Wash and dry parsley, cut off stems and fry parsley leaves in small bunches until crisp. Reserve remaining lard for roasting. • Wash lemon in hot water, dry and cut in wedges. • Arrange on warm serving dish, garnished with parsley and lemon wedges. • Serve with a green salad and potato salad.

Stuffed Chicken Legs

Slightly more difficult, but economical

450 calories per serving
Preparation time: 20 minutes
Cooking time: 45 minutes

8 chicken legs weighing 6 oz. each
¾ cup button mushrooms
Bunch parsley
2 cloves garlic
3 tbs. butter
½ tsp. lemon juice
½ tsp. salt
Pinch freshly ground white pepper
2 tbs. oil

Clean and wipe mushrooms. Wash and dry parsley, then remove stalks. Peel garlic. • Put mushrooms, parsley, garlic, butter and lemon juice in blender and blend to a smooth paste. • Preheat oven to 475°F. • Wash and dry chicken legs. Loosen skin from meat, working from thick end and pushing skin up towards bone. Spread filling over meat and pull skin down over it again. Rub pieces well with salt and pepper, brush with oil and lay on rack over roasting pan. Roast for 45 minutes in center of oven. • Serve with roast potatoes prepared in the following way: peel and halve potatoes, put in roasting pan and scatter over mixture of chopped fresh thyme, salt and oil. Place rack with chicken legs above potatoes so that fat and juices drip down and flavor them.

Chicken Strudel

Somewhat complicated, Austrian specialty

710 calories per serving
Preparation time: 1½ hours
Baking time: 30 minutes

| 2 chickens weighing 2¼ lbs. |
| 1 cup bacon |
| 2 tsp. salt |
| 2 pinches freshly ground white pepper |
| 1 tsp. dried thyme |
| 1 tsp. dried sage |
| 1 cup button mushrooms |
| 10 large leaves savoy cabbage |
| 2 eggs |
| 2 tbs. freshly chopped parsley |
| 1 cup cream |
| 1 tbs. clarified butter |
| For the pastry: |
| 2¼ cups flour |
| 1 egg |
| 2 pinches salt |
| ⅓ cup lukewarm water |
| 1 tbs. oil |
| Flour for rolling out |
| 6 tbs. clarified butter for glaze |

Skin chickens, remove breast portions and put to one side. Bone what is left and cut meat into small pieces. • Cut any remaining fat and skin from 2 livers, then wash, dry and chop. • Cut bacon in ½ in. strips. Put prepared chicken and bacon on a plate, sprinkle with salt, pepper, thyme and sage, then leave in refrigerator for 30 minutes. • Clean, wipe and slice mushrooms thinly. Wash cabbage leaves, cutting away thick stems. • Sieve flour onto pastry board, add egg, salt, and half amount of water and knead to smooth dough, adding more water if necessary. When kneaded sufficiently, the pastry should have a dull sheen. Shape into a ball, brush with oil, invert a bowl over pastry and leave to rest for 30 minutes. • Finely chop chilled chicken and bacon (still keeping breasts apart). • Put chopped meat into bowl set in another bowl containing ice cubes. Combine thoroughly with eggs, parsley and cream, season well with salt and pepper, cover and put in refrigerator for another 30 minutes.

• Melt 1 tbs. clarified butter. Cut chicken breasts in 1 in. wide strips before frying together with chopped liver over high heat for 2 minutes, turning constantly. Put to one side. • Roll out dough on floured surface into large, paper thin rectangle. Cut off any thick edges and brush with melted clarified butter all over. • Preheat oven to 400°F. • Spread cabbage leaves with one half of chopped meat, arrange chicken strips and liver along middle. Cover with remaining chopped meat, then arrange on pastry and roll it up. • Lift pastry roll onto baking sheet in the form of a horseshoe, then brush with melted butter. • Bake for 30 minutes in center of oven, brushing several times during baking with remaining melted butter. • Cut chicken strudel in 16 equal pieces and serve while still hot. • A fresh mixed salad complements this dish very well.

Confit De Canard

Specialty from France requiring time in preparation

1200 calories per serving
Preparation time: 40 minutes
Cooling time: 48 hours
Cooking time: 1-2 hours

2 plump ducks weighing 4½ lbs. each
½ cup sea salt
1 tsp. freshly ground white pepper
1 tsp. dried thyme
½ cup lard

Draw ducks, if applicable, then cut in 8 pieces each. Wash and dry them, removing and setting aside any fat. • Mix salt with pepper and thyme and rub well into duck portions. Put into large earthenware jar, sprinkle with remaining seasoning mix, cover and leave in a cool place for 24 hours. • Render duck fat down in large, heavy bottom skillet together with melted lard. Lay duck portions carefully into hot fat before covering and simmering gently (rather than frying) for 1-2 hours. After 1 hour, test meat by inserting a skewer into thickest part of thigh. If juices run out clear, the duck is cooked. • Take cooked meat off bone, put in layers into the well-washed earthenware jar and pour cooled fat over it. The fat should cover the duck by a good 1 in. After 24 hours, cover earthenware jar with aluminum foil and a lid, or a plate with a stone as weight; place in cool basement or refrigerator. • If only part of the duck is used at one time, the fat must be melted down again and poured over the remaining confit. It will keep in this way for about 10 weeks. • Prepare the duck portions for a meal by roasting in the oven at 400°F. until crisp and brown. • Serve accompanied by red cabbage with chestnuts and potato croquettes.

Stuffed Chicken with Brussels Sprouts

Requires certain amount of time

1000 calories per serving
Preparation time: 30 minutes
Cooking time: 1¼ hour

| 1 frying chicken weighing 3¼ lbs. |
| 1 large onion |
| 2 oz. bacon |
| 7 oz. chicken livers |
| 2 tbs. butter |
| 1 tart apple |
| 1 tsp. chopped mint |
| 2 tbs. fresh breadcrumbs |
| 1 tsp. salt |
| ½ tsp. white pepper |
| 4½ cups Brussels sprouts |
| ⅓ cup dry white wine |
| ¾ cup cream |
| Pinch grated nutmeg |

Wash and dry chicken. Peel onion, and finely dice. Dice bacon and washed liver. Heat 1 tbs. butter, fry chopped bacon and onion until browned, add liver and fry for 1 minute longer, then cool slightly. • Peel, core and grate apple. Combine with mint, breadcrumbs and liver mixture, season with salt and pepper. • Preheat oven to 400°F. • Season chicken with salt and pepper both inside and out before filling with stuffing and sewing up openings. • Sprinkle remaining melted butter over chicken, place in roasting pan or heavy casserole with lid and cook for 20 minutes. • Clean and wash Brussels sprouts. • Pour wine and cream over chicken, add sprouts, season with salt and nutmeg. Cook for 30 minutes longer before removing lid and allowing chicken to brown during final 25 minutes or so of cooking time.

Broiled Chicken with Mango Butter

Easy to prepare

710 calories per serving
Preparation time: 30 minutes
Chilling time: 2 hours
Cooking time: 30 minutes

| 1 chicken weighing 3¼ lbs. |
| ½ cup softened butter |
| 3 tsp. mango chutney |
| Juice of ½ lime |
| Pinch cayenne pepper |
| 2 tbs. oil |
| ½ tsp. salt |
| 2 pinches freshly ground white pepper |

Combine butter with mango chutney, lime juice and cayenne pepper, blending well. Shape into a roll, wrap in foil or wax paper and chill for about 2 hours in freezer or freezing compartment of refrigerator. • Preheat electric broiler. • Cut chicken in 8 pieces, wash and dry them, then brush lightly with oil and season with salt and pepper. • Broil chicken for 30 minutes, turning at least twice and brushing again with oil. • Divide chilled mango butter in 8 equal rounds and lay one on each portion of hot broiled chicken. • Serve with curried rice salad, fresh pita bread and a salad of avocado and tomato, or sliced fresh mango.

Tip: If you have no separate electric broiler, the chicken can be cooked either under the broiler in the oven, or on a rack in the oven with both top and bottom elements switched on.

Sesame Chicken

Wholefood recipe

520 calories per serving
Preparation time: 30 minutes
Cooking time: approx. 1 hour

| 1 chicken weighing 2¼ lbs. |
| ¼ cup sesame seeds |
| 2 tbs. sesame oil |
| 2 tbs. butter |
| 1 heaping tbs. cracked or bulgured wheat |
| 3 pinches each, salt and freshly ground white pepper |
| 1 egg |
| 1 tbs. chopped parsley |

Peel and finely chop onion. • Brown half amount of sesame seeds in skillet without any fat, then add 1 tbs. each of oil and butter. Fry chopped onion and cracked wheat or bulgured wheat briefly, turning frequently. Remove skillet from heat and stir in pinch of salt and pepper, cool slightly before mixing in egg and parsley. • Preheat oven to 425°F. • Wash and dry chicken, put stuffing into cavity and sew up openings. • Combine remaining salt and pepper with other half of sesame seeds and coat chicken with mixture, rubbing in well. • Heat remaining oil with butter, brush chicken with half of it and lay, breast downwards, in roasting pan. Roast for 25 minutes in oven, then turn breast upwards and continue to roast for 25 minutes longer. • Brush with rest of fat before roasting for final 10 or 15 minutes, basting several times with cooking juices. • Leave chicken to rest for 10 minutes in oven once it has been turned off.

Chicken with Thyme

Wholefood recipe

400 calories per serving
Preparation time: 30 minutes
Cooking time: 1 hour

| 1 chicken weighing 2¼ lbs. |
| 3 tbs. boiling milk |
| 1 heaping tbs. cracked wheat or bulgured wheat |
| 1 leek, white part only (2 oz) |
| 2 tbs. butter |
| 1 tbs. freshly chopped parsley |
| 2 tbs. dried thyme |
| 1½ tsp. sea salt |
| ½ tsp. black pepper |
| 1 egg |

Pour hot milk over cracked wheat, cover and leave to swell. • Wash leek and finely chop before browning gently in 1 tbs. butter. Add parsley and sauté briefly as well. Stir in soaked wheat and milk; bring to a boil. Cool stuffing slightly before mixing in 1 tsp. rubbed thyme, ½ tsp. salt, 1 pinch pepper and egg. • Preheat oven to 425°F. • Wash and dry chicken inside and out, put stuffing into cavity and sew up openings. • Combine remaining thyme with rest of salt and pepper, rub well into chicken skin. • Turn chicken breast upwards and continue to roast for 25 minutes longer. • Roast for final 10 minutes, basting frequently with cooking juices. • Leave for 10 minutes in oven once it has been switched off.

Masala Chicken

Specialty from India

930 calories per serving
Preparation time: 20 minutes
Marinating time: 2 hours
Cooking time: 50 minutes

2 chickens, each weighing 2¼ lbs.
2 walnut-sized pieces fresh ginger
2 cloves garlic
1 tsp. salt
½ tsp. ground cardamon
½ tsp. ground cinnamon
½ tsp. cayenne pepper
2 tbs. lemon juice
¾ cup full cream yogurt
½ cup blanched almonds
⅓ cup seedless raisins
1 tbs. butter
¾ cup water

Peel ginger and garlic, place in blender with salt, cardamon, cinnamon, cayenne pepper and lemon juice; blend to a smooth paste. • Wash and dry chickens, cut in half and lay, cut side down, in heavy metal skillet. Spread masala paste over them. • Blend yogurt with almonds and washed raisins, then pour this mixture over chickens. • Melt butter and sprinkle over chickens. Cover with aluminum foil and leave to marinate for 2 hours at room temperature. • Preheat oven to 400°F. • Pour ⅓ cup water round chickens, cover and cook for 20 minutes in oven. Reduce temperature to 325°F., remove foil and roast in chicken water if desired. • Serve chickens in the sauce, accompanied by risotto prepared with saffron and paprika.

Honey-Glazed Chicken

Easy to prepare and economical

690 calories per serving
Preparation time: 10 minutes
Cooking time: 50 minutes

2 frying chickens each weighing 2¼ lbs.
2 tsp. oil
2 tbs. runny honey
1 tbs. medium hot mustard
2 tsp. curry powder
½ tsp salt

Preheat oven to 425°F. Wash, dry and halve chickens. Cut 4 pieces of aluminum foil large enough to wrap half of the chicken. Brush with oil and lay chicken halves cut side down on foil. • Combine honey with mustard, curry powder and salt; brush chicken with this mixture.

Wrap foil loosely around chicken, sealing edges well. • Put foil parcels on roasting rack and cook in center of oven for 30 minutes. At end of this time, open foil and continue to cook for 20 minutes longer until skin is crisp and brown. • Serve chicken with peanut rice or french fries and a fresh mixed salad.

Chicken Wings in Batter

Economical

600 calories per serving
Standing time for batter: 30 minutes
Total preparation time: 1 hour

12 chicken wings
¾ cup flour
½ tsp. salt
Good pinch cayenne pepper
2 eggs
⅓ cup beer
1 tbs. oil
For frying:
4 cups oil or 4½ cups lard

Combine flour, salt and cayenne pepper. Separate egg yolks from whites. Beat yolks with beer and oil, then stir into dry ingredients. Set batter aside for 30 minutes. • Heat oil or lard to 350°F. in deep-fryer with thermometer. Preheat oven to 200°F. • Wash and dry chicken wings. • Beat egg whites until stiff and fold into batter. • Dip chicken wings in batter before frying a few at a time in deep fat for about 4 minutes on each side until crisp and golden. • Drain on absorbent paper towel, then keep warm on dish in oven until all are done. • Serve garnished with wedges of lemon and fresh parsley, accompanied by potato salad with fresh herbs and radishes.

Deep-Fried Chicken

Economical

760 calories per serving
Total preparation time: 1½ hours

2 chickens, each weighing 1 lb. 6 oz.
½ cup flour
2 tsp. salt
2 eggs
5 tbs. mineral water
½ tsp. freshly ground white pepper
For frying:
4 cups coconut oil or 4½ cups clarified butter

Mix flour and salt to batter with eggs and mineral water, then cover and leave to stand for 20 minutes. • Cut chickens in 8 pieces each before washing and drying them. • Heat fat to 350°F. in deep-fryer with thermometer. Heat oven to 200°F. • Dip chicken pieces one by one in batter and fry a few at a time in fat until crisp and brown, about 8 minutes on each side. Drain chicken pieces on absorbent paper towel before keeping warm on plate in oven. Season with salt and pepper before serving. • Delicious accompanied by a salad of tiny raw peas and sweetcorn with crusty French bread.

Tip: This recipe can equally well be followed using chicken breasts or drumsticks, which are often sold quite cheaply.

Chicken Stuffed with Sweetbreads

More expensive and time-consuming

1200 calories per serving
Preparation time: 45 minutes
Cooking time: 1¼ hours

1 chicken weighing 3¼ lbs.
1 tsp. salt
1 tsp. dried tarragon
½ tsp. white pepper
9 oz. sweetbreads (brains)
1 cup button mushrooms
2 shallots
1 clove garlic
¼ lb. beef marrow
1 tbs. freshly chopped parsley
2 tbs. brandy
2 tbs. fresh breadcrumbs
1 egg
¼ cup butter
½ cup dry white wine
1¾ cups sour cream

Wash and dry chicken, then rub well inside with salt and tarragon, outside with pepper. • Wash sweetbreads, cut off any fat or membrane, soak for 10 minutes to remove any remaining blood, then cube. • Clean and wash mushrooms, then thinly slice. Peel and finely chop shallots and garlic. • Combine marrow with sweetbreads, mushrooms, shallots, garlic, parsley, brandy, breadcrumbs and egg, seasoning to taste with salt and pepper. Stuff chicken with mixture and sew up openings. • Preheat oven to 400°F. • Heat butter in heavy bottomed pan. Brown chicken thoroughly on all sides over high heat before turning on its back and roasting on lowest shelf of oven for 1¼ hours. • During roasting, baste frequently with wine and cooking juices. • Allow cooked chicken to rest on wire rack in oven. • Meanwhile, put cooking juices into small saucepan, scraping out any brown crusty bits, mix with sour cream and simmer, stirring well, until sauce is reduced by half.

Guinea Fowl with Lentil Puree

Rather expensive

1400 calories per serving
Preparation time: 15 minutes
Cooking time: 50 minutes

---

4 guinea fowl, each weighing
1¾ pounds

---

1 onion

---

1 clove garlic

---

2 oz. bacon

---

5 tbs. oil

2¼ cups red lentils

---

1 cup red wine

---

1 cup water

2¼ cup sour cream

---

1 bay leaf

---

1 tsp. salt

---

1 tsp. freshly ground black
pepper

---

3 crushed juniper berries

---

4 thin strips fatty bacon

Bunch fresh basil

---

1 egg

Peel onion and garlic, chop finely with first quantity of bacon and sauté in 2 tbs. oil. Add lentils, ½ cup red wine, water, sour cream and bay leaf. Cover and simmer for about 10 minutes until soft. • Wash and dry guinea fowl, season with salt and pepper and rub well with juniper berries. Cover breast of each bird with 1 bacon strip and truss. • Preheat oven to 425°F. • Brown guinea fowl in remaining oil before roasting for 20 minutes in oven. • Pour over remaining red wine and continue cooking guinea fowl for 30 minutes longer. • Remove bacon after 20 minutes of this time. • Meanwhile, discard bay leaf and purée lentils. • Chop basil finely and stir into purée with egg, salt and pepper. • Carve guinea fowl

and serve on bed of lentil purée, garnished with basil leaves.

Partridge with Savoy Cabbage

Rather expensive

1100 calories per serving
Preparation time: 1 hour
Cooking time: 30 minutes

---

4 partridges, each weighing
1¼ lbs.

---

1 tsp. salt

---

1 tsp. freshly ground black
pepper

¼ cup clarified butter

4½ cups savoy cabbage

---

1 tsp. dried marjoram

---

1 bay leaf

---

2 cloves

---

1 cup small onions

---

1 large carrot

¼ lb. lean bacon

Wash and dry partridges, then rub well with salt and pepper • Heat 2 tbs. clarified butter and sear partridges thoroughly. Add 3 tbs. water, cover and cook very gently for 15 minutes. • Quarter cabbage and remove hard core before chopping coarsely. Sauté briefly in 1 tbs. clarified butter, add 3 tbs. water, marjoram, bay leaf and 1 peeled onion with clove-spiked bay leaf; cover and braise for 20 minutes till tender. • Cut partridges in half. • Peel remaining onions, and carrot, dice both with bacon and sauté in remaining clarified butter. • Preheat oven to 400°F. • Put half cabbage into large ovenproof dish, place halved partridges on top, sprinkle with bacon mixture and finish off with remaining cabbage. Pour cooking juices from game over dish, seal well with foil and cook in oven for 30 minutes longer.

Stuffed Guinea Fowl

Rather more expensive

950 calories per serving
Preparation time: 30 minutes
Cooking time: 50 minutes

2 guinea fowl, each weighing 1¾ lbs.:
1 cup mushrooms
2 oz. lean bacon
1 tsp. butter
7 oz. chicken livers
1 small onion
¼ cup brandy
1 tsp. dried tarragon
1 tsp. salt
1 tsp. freshly ground white pepper
2 tbs. breadcrumbs
Small quantity soup vegetables
¼ cup oil
1 cup dry red wine
1 small bay leaf
½ cup cream

Clean, wash and drain mushrooms before thinly slicing.
• Dice bacon, brown in butter together with mushrooms and cool. • Wash and finely chop liver. Peel and dice onion, then mix with liver, brandy, tarragon, ½ tsp. salt, ½ tsp. pepper and breadcrumbs. Combine this mixture with mushrooms and bacon. • Wash and dry guinea fowl, fill cavities with stuffing and sew up. • Preheat oven to 400°F. • Rub remaining salt and pepper well into guinea fowl. Clean and finely chop soup vegetables. • Heat oil in large, heavy bottomed pan and sauté guinea fowl for 10 minutes. Pour off oil. Lay birds in pan again on their backs, add soup vegetables and roast in oven for 10 minutes. • Pour on half red wine and add bay leaf. • After 30 minutes more, gradually add remaining red wine, basting birds frequently with cooking juices. • Brown guinea fowl on wire rack in oven for 10 minutes longer. • Strain cooking juices, combine with cream and reduce by half.

Stuffed Turkey with Chestnut Sauce

Very popular recipe

1500 calories per serving
Preparation time: 45 minutes
Cooking time: 2½ hours

1 turkey weighing 6½ lbs.
1 tsp. salt
1 tsp. freshly ground white pepper
1 tsp. mild paprika
3 tart apples
1¾ cups chopped hazelnuts
½ cup marzipan
2 pinches cinnamon
Juice of ½ lemon
1 cup hot chicken broth
⅓ cup butter
½ cup white wine
¾ cup chestnut purée (canned)
1¾ cups cream
2 tbs. brandy
Oil for brushing roasting pan

Preheat oven to 400°F. Brush roasting pan with oil. • Wash and dry turkey, rub well inside with salt, pepper and paprika. • Quarter apples, then peel, core and dice them. Combine two-thirds of apple with nuts, finely-chopped marzipan, cinnamon and 1 tbs. lemon juice. Stuff turkey with this mixture. Sew up openings and truss turkey. • Sprinkle remaining lemon juice on rest of diced apple. • Roast turkey breast side down in oven for 1 hour, basting occasionally with chicken stock. • Turn turkey over and continue to roast for 1½ hours longer. • Put turkey on meat dish and leave to stand in oven for 15 minutes once it has been switched off. • Melt butter and combine with diced apple. Strain cooking juices and mix with white wine, chestnut purée, diced apple and cream, seasoning to taste with brandy, salt, pepper and cinnamon. • Serve accompanied by red cabbage and potato fritters.

Chicken with Dried Fruit

Requires certain amount of time

1000 calories per serving
Preparation time: 40 minutes
Cooking time: 1¼ hours

1 chicken weighing 3 lbs.
¾ cup stoned prunes
¾ cup dried apricots
1 tbs. raisins
1½ cups water
4 zweiback biscuits
3 tbs. pouring cream
1 egg
2 tbs. brandy
1 tart apple
2 tsp. mild paprika
2 pinches each white pepper and salt
3 tbs. clarified butter
Small quantity soup vegetables
1¾ cups sour cream

Bring dried fruit and water to a boil, then drain, reserving water. • Crumble zweibacks and mix with cream, egg and brandy. • Peel, core and dice apple, before combining it with dried fruit and zweiback mixture. • Preheat oven to 400°F. • Wash and dry chicken; rub both inside and out with paprika and pepper, salting inside only. • Fill chicken with fruit stuffing, sew up, truss (p.), place in roasting pan and pour melted clarified butter over. Roast for 1¼ hours. • Wash and chop soup vegetables, then simmer in reserved cooking water with chopped giblets for 30 minutes. Strain broth at end of this time. • Keep chicken warm. • Deglaze roasting pan with broth, stir in sour cream and boil until smooth and slightly thickened.

Chicken in Cider

Specialty from Normandy

900 calories per serving
Preparation time: 30 minutes
Cooking time: 45 minutes

1 chicken weighing 3¼ lbs.
1 tsp. salt
½ tsp. white pepper
½ cup butter
1 cup dry cider
3 cups carrots
1 tbs. honey
¼ cup freshly chopped parsley
½ cup cream
Bunch fresh tarragon

Cut chicken in 8 pieces, wash and dry, then rub well with salt and pepper. • Heat half the butter in heavy bottomed pan, sear chicken pieces, add cider and cover before braising for 45 minutes. • Peel, wash and dry carrots; cut in 2 in. pieces. Heat remaining butter in deep pan, add carrots with a little salt and ¼ cup water, cover and steam gently for 20 minutes. Allow any remaining water to evaporate, glaze carrots with honey and sprinkle with 1 tbs. parsley before covering and keeping warm. • Arrange chicken pieces on warm serving dish. Reduce sauce by half over high heat, then stir in cream, remaining parsley and chopped tarragon. Taste and adjust seasoning if necessary. • Serve chicken with sauce and carrots, completing the meal with parsley potatoes.

Pigeons with Brown Rice

Wholefood recipe

880 calories per serving
Total preparation time: 1 hour

4 pigeons, each weighing 10 oz.
1 cup long grain brown rice
2 tsp. sea salt
1 tsp. black pepper
¼ cup softened butter
¾ cup cream
½ cup dry white wine
1 large onion (9 oz.)
3 cups cucumber
2 tbs. butter
2 pinches seasoning salt
1 pinch white pepper
2 tbs. fresh dill

Bring rice to boil with 2 cups water and set aside. • Preheat oven to 425°F. • Wash pigeons, rub well inside and out with salt and pepper, then spread with thick layer of softened butter. • Put into roasting pan breast side down and roast for 20 minutes. Place pot of rice in bottom of oven. • Turn pigeons over after 20 minutes, pour cream over and roast for 10 minutes more, basting frequently with cooking juices. • Finally pour in white wine. • Switch off oven and leave pigeons there for 10 minutes. • Meanwhile, peel and finely chop onion. Wash cucumber and cut in julienne strips. Sauté both gently in butter until transparent, adding seasoning salt and pepper to taste. Continue to cook gently for about 15 minutes until cucumber is done, then combine with rice, cooking juices and dill and spoon onto serving dish. Arrange pigeons on top.

Chicken with Cold Nut Sauce

Very well-known recipe

740 calories per serving
Preparation time: 30 minutes
Cooking time: 1 hour

1 chicken weighing 3 lbs.
1 tsp. curry powder
1 tsp. mild paprika
Pinch freshly ground white pepper
1 tsp. salt
3 tbs. sunflower oil
For the nut sauce:
2 slices wholewheat bread
½ cup shelled walnuts
1 clove garlic
3 tbs. walnut oil
1 tsp. red wine vinegar
¼ tsp. honey
2 pinches salt

Preheat oven to 400°F. • Wash and dry chicken. • Combine all spices with salt and rub inside of chicken with mixture. Truss, brush with sunflower oil, lay breast down in roasting pan and roast for 1 hour in oven. • Turn chicken over after 30 minutes and baste frequently with cooking juices. • Switch off oven and allow chicken to stand for 10 minutes. • Cube bread and soak in ½ cup water. Grind walnuts. Squeeze bread dry and rub through sieve, then combine with ground nuts. Peel and finely chop garlic. Stir walnut oil, vinegar, 2 tbs. water and garlic into bread and nut mixture, season with honey and salt. Serve with neatly carved slices of chicken.

Pigeon Pie

Rather complicated, specialty from Morocco

945 calories per serving
Standing time: 6 hours
Preparation time: 1½ hours
Cooking time: 1 hour

6 pigeons, each weighing 14 oz.	
2¼ cups flour	
2½ tsp. salt	
1½-2cups litre water	
½ tsp. white pepper	
4 onions	
¼ cup clarified butter	
2 tbs. freshly chopped parsley	
2 tbs. freshly grated green ginger	
1 tsp. grated lemon rind (organically grown)	
½ tsp. ground caraway	
1 pinch cayenne pepper	
¼ tsp. powdered saffron	
1 pinch tumeric	

½ cup white wine	
½ cup water	
6 eggs	
2 egg yolks	
¾ cup coarsely chopped almonds	
3 tbs. butter	
½ tsp. cinnamon	
1 tbs. sugar	
2 tbs. oil	
For dusting over pie:	
Icing sugar and cinnamon	

To make the batter, sieve flour into bowl, add 1 tsp. salt and enough water to mix to a smooth, almost runny consistency. Cover and leave for 6 hours. • Wash and dry pigeons; season with salt and pepper. Wash, dry and finely chop giblets. Peel and chop onions. • Heat clarified butter in large, heavy bottomed pan with lid; brown pigeons thoroughly, then remove from pan. Sauté onion and giblets in remaining fat, add parsley and all spices, (except cinnamon). Stir in wine and water and bring to a boil. • Put pigeons carefully into boiling broth, cover and simmer for 1 hour. • Lift out pigeons, cool slightly, take meat off bone and cut in fine strips. • Pour half of broth into another saucepan. Boil remainder rapidly until reduced to ¼ cup, then cool and skim off fat. • Heat up other half of broth to just below boiling point. Whisk eggs with yolks and pour into hot broth, taking care not to boil, but to stir continuously. Add reduced broth as well. • Brown almonds carefully in 1 tbs. butter, stirring constantly; remove from pan and cool, then mix with sugar and cinnamon. • Using a non-stick frying pan without any fat, make batter into 18 paper-thin, golden brown pancakes. • To form pie crust, take a double layer of foil, lay on it 6 pancakes overlapping in a circle the same size as large frying pan. Cover with second layer of 6 pancakes. Place almonds in center of round, then combine pigeon with egg sauce and pour over almonds, leaving about 3 in. free around edges. Brush edges lightly with melted butter and fold as far as possible over filling. Cover with remaining 6 pancakes. • Heat oil with remaining butter in large frying pan. Slide pie carefully off foil and into pan; fry gently for 10 minutes until nicely browned. • Turn pie with help of frying pan lid to brown other side, again for 10 minutes. • Combine icing sugar and cinnamon and sieve over pie. • Serve with a colorful mixed salad.

Quail Stuffed with Morels

A classic, rather expensive, recipe

570 calories per serving
Preparation time: 45 minutes
Cooking time: 30 minutes

6 quails, each weighing 7 oz.
2 tbs. dried morels (small brown mushrooms)
¼ cup dry sherry
1 slice bread
2 tbs. cream
1 shallot
1 bunch chervil
1 tsp. salt
½ tsp. white pepper
9 oz. sausage meat
Pinch nutmeg
1 tbs. oil
2 tbs. butter
1 cup cream

Soak morels in sherry. • Cut crusts off bread, cube and sprinkle with 2 tbs. cream. • Bone quails, apart from wings and legs. • Peel and finely chop shallot. Wash, dry and finely chop chervil. • Rub each quail well with 1 pinch salt and chopped shallot. Combine sausage meat, chervil, nutmeg, soft bread, remaining salt and pepper with morels, left whole and without sherry. • Stuff quails with this mixture and truss. • Preheat oven to 425°F. • Heat oil and butter in large frying pan. Brown quails in this before putting into roasting pan, pouring over remaining fat, sherry and cream and roasting on lowest shelf of oven for 30 minutes. • At end of this time, switch off heat and leave quail in oven for 5 minutes longer. • Serve with champagne sauerkraut and mashed potato.

Chicken with Sweet Corn Stuffing

Economical and easy to prepare

980 calories per serving
Preparation time: 45 minutes
Cooking time: 1¼ hours

1 chicken weighing 3¼ lbs.
2 cobs sweet corn
1½ tsp. salt
1 green pepper
2 tbs. butter
¼ lb. sausage meat
½ tsp. white pepper
2 tbs. oil
1 carrot
1 onion
1 clove garlic
5 tbs. white wine
5 tbs. chicken broth
1 cup sour cream

Cover sweet corn with water, add ½ tsp. salt and boil for 45 minutes. Scrape kernels off cob. • Wash and dry chicken; chop heart and liver. • Preheat oven to 400°F. • Clean and dice green pepper, then sauté in 1 tbs. butter with giblets. Add sausage meat and sweet corn kernels, seasoning well. • Stuff chicken with this mixture, sew up, brush with oil and roast for 1¼ hours on lowest shelf of oven. • Peel and grate carrot. Peel onion and cut in eighths. Peel and chop garlic, sauté in remaining butter with carrot and onion until nicely browned, pour in wine and broth and simmer for 10 minutes. Strain and combine with sour cream.

Turkey Breasts in Puff Pastry

Slightly more expensive and complicated

900 calories per serving
Preparation time: 40 minutes
Cooking time: 30 minutes

6 boneless turkey breasts, each weighing 6 oz.
2½ cups frozen puff pastry
¼ cup butter
Finely ground beef steak
1 cup cream
2 eggs
3 tbs. freshly chopped mixed herbs (including chervil, parsley and sage)
½ tsp. salt
½ tsp. freshly ground black pepper
½ tsp. mild paprika
Pinch nutmeg
¾ cup ground hazelnuts
1 egg yolk
2 tbs. milk
Flour for rolling out

Remove pastry from wrappings and thaw. • Wash and dry turkey breasts, brown well in butter, remove from pan and allow to cool. • Combine ground beef with cream, eggs and herbs; season well with salt, pepper, paprika and nutmeg. • Coat turkey breasts with thick layer of this mixture. • Preheat oven to 400°F. • Roll thawed pastry out slightly on floured work surface, sprinkle with hazelnuts then continue to roll out until ½ in. thick. • Cut pastry in squares to fit turkey breasts. Place one turkey breast on each square, brush edges with water, fold round meat and seal well. • Place pastry parcels on cold baking sheet that has been rinsed in cold water and left wet. • Brush pastry with beaten egg and milk. • Bake on middle shelf of oven for 30 minutes.

American Thanksgiving Turkey

Specialty from America, requiring some time for preparation

1200 calories per serving
Preparation time: 1 hour
Cooking time: 3-3½ hours

1 young turkey weighing 9 lbs.
2½ tsp. salt
1½-2 tsp. freshly ground white pepper
Bunch parsley
1 lemon
2 onions
½ cup butter
6 slices bread
½ cup milk
2 eggs
2 tsp. dried sage
½ bouillon cube
1 tsp. curry powder
3 cups bouillon
3½ cups sweet potatoes (canned yams)
2 rounded tbs. sugar
2 tbs. cornstarch

Wash and dry turkey inside and out; wash and dry giblets. Rub inside with 2 tsp. salt and ½-1 tsp. pepper. • Wash, dry and chop parsley. • Cut lemon in half and rub juice well into outside of turkey. • Peel onions, then chop with liver. • Melt half the butter in pan and sauté onion and liver with parsley. Cube bread and combine with onion and liver mix, milk, eggs, sage, remaining pepper and salt and bouillion. • Preheat oven to 325°F. • Stuff turkey with mixture and sew up openings, then truss. • Put turkey into roasting pan. Melt remaining butter, stir in curry powder and brush bird all over with this mixture. Use some to grease piece of kitchen foil and place over turkey. Put on bottom shelf of oven and roast for 3–3½ hours. • At end of 1½ hours, add gizzard, heart and neck, pour on a little hot bouillon, just enough to keep moist, and baste turkey frequently with cooking juices. • Test to see if done after 3 hours by piercing thickest part of leg with skewer. The juices will run clear when turkey is cooked. Once cooked, remove turkey from oven and allow to stand, covered with foil. • Turn oven up to 425°F. • Drain sweet potatoes, put into ovenproof dish, sprinkle with sugar and bake in center of oven for 20 minutes until well browned. • Carve turkey and arrange on warm meat dish with sweet potatoes. Keep warm in oven once switched off. • Pour off fat from roasting pan. Discard gizzard, but chop heart and meat from neck finely. • Deglaze roasting pan with remaining stock, pour into small saucepan and bring to boil. Add finely chopped meat. Mix cornstarch to paste with 2 tbs. water and thicken sauce with this. Taste for seasoning and serve with turkey. • Additional accompaniments are cranberry sauce and buttered green peas.

Pheasant in Bacon Sauce

Rather expensive

1000 calories per serving
Preparation time: 40 minutes
Cooking time: 40 minutes

1 pheasant weighing 2¾ lbs.
1½ tsp. salt
½ tsp. black pepper
4 thin strips fatty bacon
¼ cup butter
2 oz. lean bacon
1 carrot
¾ cup leeks
Bunch parsley
2 juniper berries
2 tbs. oil
5 peppercorns
2 cups water
½ cup grape juice
3 tbs. dry sherry
½ cup sour cream

Preheat oven to 425°F. •
Wash and dry pheasant. Cut off wings and rub well inside with pepper and 1 tsp. salt. • Cover breast with bacon strips and tie in place. • Heat butter in roasting pan. Brown pheasant well all over, turn breast down and slide onto bottom oven shelf. Roast for 40 minutes. • Remove bacon 10 minutes before end of roasting time, turn pheasant over on back and brown breast. • To make the sauce, dice both lots of bacon; peel, wash and chop carrot; clean and split leeks lengthwise, then wash and slice. Chop parsley and crush juniper berries. • Heat oil. Sauté bacon, then pheasant wings and giblets as well. Add prepared vegetables, parsley, juniper berries, ½ tsp. salt, peppercorns and water; boil for 20 minutes. • Strain sauce through sieve. • Keep pheasant warm. • Deglaze roasting pan with sauce, pour into saucepan, add sherry and grape juice and reduce to 1 cup. Stir in sour cream.

Stuffed Pheasant

Somewhat more expensive

880 calories per serving
Preparation time: 20 minutes
Cooking time: 40 minutes

1 pheasant weighing 2¾ lbs.
¼ lb. Parma ham
3 oz. lean bacon
6 leaves fresh sage
1 tsp. salt
½ tsp. black pepper
½ tsp. grated lemon rind (organically grown)
¼ cup olive oil
4 thin strips fatty bacon
½ cup dry white wine

Wash and dry pheasant. Dice lean bacon and Parma ham finely. Chop sage and combine with a little salt, pepper, lemon rind and diced bacon and ham. • Preheat oven to 425°F. • Rub pheasant inside with salt, then fill with stuffing and sew up. • Heat oil in roasting pan. Brown pheasant well on all sides, lay on back in pan and cover breast with bacon strips. • Roast pheasant on lowest oven shelf for 40 minutes, basting frequently with wine and pan juices. Remove bacon 10 minutes before end of roasting time to allow breast to brown.

Breast of Turkey with Yogurt Sauce

Specialty from Bulgaria

430 calories per serving
Preparation time: 40 minutes
Cooking time: 45 minutes

2¼ lbs. turkey breast on bone
2 cloves garlic
½ tsp. salt
2 pinches freshly ground black pepper
6 tbs. sunflower oil
1 yellow and 1 red pepper
1 cup leeks
2¼ cup cucumber
Bunch chervil
½ cup hot chicken broth
1¼ cup full cream yogurt

Wash and dry turkey breast. • Peel and chop garlic, mix with salt and pepper, then crush and combine with 1 tbs. oil. Coat meat with this mixture before covering and putting in refrigerator to marinate for 30 minutes. • Preheat oven to 400°F. • Discard stalk and seeds of peppers, wash and chop. Trim both ends of leeks, wash thoroughly and cut in ½ in. pieces. Peel and dice cucumber. Wash, dry and finely chop chervil. • Heat remaining oil. Place turkey breast in roasting pan, pour hot oil over and roast in center of oven for 30 minutes. Arrange chopped peppers and leek around meat, pour on hot broth and cook for 10 minutes longer. Finally add cucumber and cook for 5 more minutes. • Remove meat and vegetables from pan, put on warm serving dish and return to oven once switched off to keep warm. • Deglaze roasting pan with yogurt, pour into sauce boat and sprinkle with chervil.

Turkey Breasts with Zucchini

Wholefood recipe that is easily prepared

430 calories per serving
Total preparation time: 40 minutes

4 boneless turkey breasts, each weighing 6 oz.
4½ cups very small zucchini
4 shallots
¼ cup sunflower oil
1 cup hot chicken broth
1 tsp. mild paprika
3 pinches white pepper
Good pinch seasoning salt
Juice of ½ lemon
2 tbs. freshly chopped parsley
2 tsp. soy sauce

Wash and dry zucchini before cutting in thick strips. Peel and halve shallots, then slice crosswise. Heat 2 tbs. oil in large pan, sauté shallots until transparent, then add zucchini, cover and braise gently for 5 minutes over low heat. Add chicken broth, season with paprika and pinch pepper, cover again almost completely, and continue to simmer for 10 minutes longer. Finally remove lid altogether and cook zucchini until almost all liquid has evaporated. • Flatten turkey slightly and rub well with remaining pepper. • Heat remaining oil in two large frying-pans and fry turkey for 2-3 minutes on each side until well browned. • Season vegetables to taste with seasoning salt and lemon juice, stir in parsley and arrange on serving dish with turkey. Sprinkle soy sauce over turkey and serve with potatoes boiled in their jackets.

Turkey Breasts with Sage

Quick and easy to make

380 calories per serving
Total preparation time: 35 minutes

8 small boneless turkey breasts, each weighing approx. 3 oz.
1 turkey liver
4 leaves fresh sage
1 large clove garlic
Piece peel from organicially grown lemon
2 oz. raw ham, without fat
3 anchovies
1 tbs. capers
¼ cup olive oil
1 tsp. salt
½ tsp. white pepper
Juice of ½ lemon

Wash and dry sage, then cut in fine strips. Peel and crush garlic. Wash turkey liver, remove any fat or membrane, then cube. Chop lemon peel, ham, anchovies and capers finely before combining with cubed liver and garlic. • Wash and dry turkey breasts. • Heat oil in two large frying-pans, put half chopped mixture in each and sauté briefly before laying 4 turkey breasts on top. Season turkey with salt, pepper and sage, sprinkle on lemon juice. Cook for 2–3 minutes on each side, then serve up on warmed plate with spicy mixture. • Rice and peas make a good accompaniment to this dish.

Roast Wild Duck

Rather more expensive

1300 calories per serving
Preparation time: 40 minutes
Cooking time: 1½ hours

1 young wild duck weighing 3¼ lbs.
1 cup mushrooms
¼ lb. lean bacon
1 onion
2 tsp. butter
1 tsp. dried tarragon
¼ cup brandy
1 tsp. salt
½ tsp. white pepper
10 oz. finely ground beef steak
½ cup fresh breadcrumbs
½ cup oil
2 apples
½ cup hot chicken broth
½ cup dry white wine

Clean, wash and thinly slice mushrooms. Dice bacon, peel onion and chop finely • Melt butter. Sauté diced bacon to remove fat, then onion until transparent, and finally mushrooms. Season with tarragon, brandy, salt and pepper. Combine this mixture with ground beef and breadcrumbs. • Preheat oven to 400°F. • Wash, dry and stuff duck, then sew up and truss. • Heat oil in roasting pan. Sear duck thoroughly, then place on bottom shelf of oven and roast for 1½ hours. • Peel, core and cut apples in eighths, adding them to roasting pan, together with chicken broth, after first 30 minutes. Pour in white wine after 1 hour and baste duck frequently with juices. • Switch off oven and leave duck in it to keep warm. Sieve cooking juices, season to taste and serve with potato dumplings and cranberry sauce.

Duck and Almonds

Rather more expensive

1400 calories per serving
Preparation time: 30 minutes
Cooking time: 1½ hours

1 duck weighing 4 lbs.
1 clove garlic
2 cups water
½ tsp. salt
1 cup dry sherry
1 onion
½ cup oil
¾ cup blanched almonds
1 tbs. cornstarch
Pinch freshly ground white pepper
Pinch sugar
¼ cup soy sauce

Wash and dry duck and giblets. Peel and quarter garlic. Cut neck and wings off duck, place in pan with water, salt, sherry, garlic and giblets and bring to a boil. • Cut duck in 4, put into boiling broth and simmer gently for 1 hour on low heat. • Strain broth, skim off fat, then reduce over high heat to 1½ cups. • Take meat off bone, retaining skin. Peel onion and slice in thin rings. • Heat oil in deep frying pan. Sauté almonds and onion until evenly brown, then remove from pan. Put pieces of duck into frying pan, skin side down, sauté until brown, then keep warm on serving dish. • Mix cornstarch to paste with cold water. Use this to thicken stock, season to taste with pepper, sugar and soy sauce. Pour over duck, garnish with onion rings and almonds.

Duck a l'Orange

One of the classic French recipes

760 calories per serving
Preparation time: 45 minutes
Cooking time: approx. 1¼ hours

1 oven-ready duck, weighing 3¼ lbs.
1 medium carrot
1 stick celery
1 medium onion
3 oranges
1 lemon
1 tsp. salt
2 pinches white pepper
2 tbs. oil
1½ cups hot chicken broth
⅓ cup sugar
¼ cup white wine vinegar
¼ cup Cointreau
2 tbs. cornstarch
2 tbs. marmalade

Wash duck thoroughly, both inside and out under cold running water, then dry well. • Peel carrot and celery under lukewarm water, then dry and cut into small pieces. Peel and dice onion. • Peel 1 orange, removing all white string; using a sharp knife, cut down between segment skins and separate pieces carefully. Peel a second orange and the lemon as thinly as possible and cut peel in julienne strips. • Preheat oven to 400°F. • Squeeze juice of lemon and 2 oranges and put to one side. • Rub duck well inside with salt and pepper and truss. • Heat oil in roasting pan in oven. When hot, lay duck breast down in pan and roast for 15 minutes. • Then put diced carrot, onion and celery into roasting pan round duck, roast duck for 15 minutes on each side. Finally turn duck over on back, pour over hot broth and bake for 25 minutes

longer on bottom shelf until done. • Meanwhile, melt sugar to a light brown in heavy bottomed pan over gently heat. Add rind and juice of citrus fruit; simmer gently for 30 minutes. • When duck is done, place on warmed dish, switch off oven and put duck back in for 10 minutes. • Pour all fat out of roasting pan, deglaze pan with vinegar, then combine with citrus syrup and simmer very gently for 1 minute. Take saucepan off heat and stir in liqueur. • Mix cornstarch to thin paste with 2 tbs. cold water, stir into sauce and bring to boil again, then stir in marmalade. Season to taste with salt and pepper. • Remove trussing string from duck before carving. Garnish with orange segments, serving sauce separately. • Serve with almond croquettes and buttered green beans.

Tip: To ensure that the sauce contains as little fat as possible, allow pan juices to cool completely so that solidified fat may be removed easily. Then reheat juices before stirring in vinegar. Keep duck warm in meantime by wrapping in double layer of foil and leaving in oven heated to 200°F.

Goose with Cranberry Sauce

Rather expensive

1410 calories per serving
Preparation time: 20 minutes
Cooking time: 2½ hours
Serves: 6 people

1 young fat goose, weighing 6½ lbs.
2 tsp. salt
1 tsp. black pepper
1 cup cranberry jelly
½ cup dry red wine
2 pinches cinnamon
2 pinches nutmeg
1 tsp. sugar

Preheat oven to 350°F. • Wash and dry goose, then rub well with salt and pepper. • Finely chop giblets. • Truss goose and lay breast down in roasting pan. Add giblets and 1 cup boil-ing water, place on bottom shelf of oven and roast for 1 hour. Then turn over and prick legs in several places to allow fat to run out. • Roast goose for 1 hour longer, basting often with pan juices and adding more boiling water if necessary. • Skim fat off juices whenever possible. • After roasting goose for 2 hours, brush several times with cold salted water. The goose is done when juices run clear when piercing thickest part of leg with skewer. • Once done, switch off oven and leave goose in it for 20 minutes. • Mix cranberry jelly with red wine, sugar and spices. Deglaze roasting pan with boiling water, strain and combine with cran-berry sauce. Bring to a boil and season to taste.

Goose Stuffed with Dried Fruit

Rather expensive

1560 calories per serving
Preparation time: 40 minutes
Cooking time: 3½ hours

1 goose weighing 9 lbs.
½ cup raisins
1 cup pitted prunes
1 cup dried figs
2 oranges
2 tsp. salt
1 tsp. black pepper

Preheat over to 350°F. • Soak raisins and prunes for 15 minutes, then drain. Wash figs in warm water, dry and dice. Wash oranges in hot water, peel very thinly and chop finely. • Wash, dry and chop liver and heart of goose, before combining with dried fruit and orange peel. • Wash and dry goose, rub well in-side with salt and pepper, then stuff with fruit mixture and sew up. • Truss goose and lay on wire rack over roasting pan. Pour 1 cup boiling water into pan and place in bottom of oven. • Roast for 3½ hours, basting frequently with pan juices. • After first hour, Turn goose over and prick legs to allow fat to run out. During next 2½ hours, brush goose fre-quently with cold salted water and skim fat off pan juices. Once done, switch off oven and leave goose in it for 20 minutes longer. • Remove pits from oranges and divide carefully into skinless seg-ments. Deglaze roasting pan with hot water and strain. Carve goose, garnish with orange seg-ments and serve sauce sepa-rately.

Traditional Christmas Goose

Requires time for preparation and cooking

1630 calories per serving
Preparation time: 1 hour
Cooking time: 4 hours

1 goose weighing 11 lbs.
3 cups sweet chestnuts
2 cups chicken broth
3 tsp. salt
1 tsp. white pepper
2¼ cups tart apples
½ cup raisins
½ tsp. dried mugwort
1 cup boiling water
1 tbs. flour
½ tsp. sugar

Preheat oven to 325°F. • Cut cross through skin of each chestnut and bake in oven until skins split open. Peel chestnuts. Bring broth to a boil, simmer chestnuts in broth for 10 minutes, then drain and cool, reserving broth. • Wash and dry goose, then rub well with salt and pepper. • Peel, quarter, core and slice apples. Wash and dry raisins before combining with apple slices, mugwort and chestnuts. Stuff goose with this mixture and sew up. • Truss goose, place breast down in roasting pan, pour boiling water over and bake in oven for about 4 hours. • After 1 hour, turn goose over and prick legs well. Then continue to bake for another 2½ hours, basting frequently with pan juices. • After 3½ hours, brush goose several times with cold salted water to make skin crisp. • Remove goose from roasting pan and place on meat dish. Switch off oven and put goose back in for 20 minutes. • Skim fat off pan juices, then deglaze pan with boiling water, strain and add water to make 2 cups. Thicken with flour mixed to thin paste with cold water. Season to taste with salt, pepper and sugar.

Cold Poultry

Turkey Parfait with Two Sauces

Excellent as first course, though rather expensive

450 calories per serving
Preparation time: 1½ hours
Chilling time: 25 minutes

14 oz. turkey liver	
14 oz. turkey breast	
2 shallots	
¼ cup butter	
1 tsp. salt	
2 pinches allspice	
2 pinches freshly ground black pepper	
2 pinches dried marjoram	
2 pinches thyme	
2 pinches sugar	
1 tbs. Armagnac or port	
5 egg whites	
3 tsp. gelatin	
1¼ cup double cream	
½ cup chicken broth	
For sauces:	
4 tart apples	
1 tbs. sugar	
Pinch cinnamon	
½ cup apple juice	
1 cup elderberry pulp (from health food shop)	
Juice of 1 lemon	
½-1 tsp. maple syrup	
Pinch salt	
Pinch cayenne pepper	

Cut all fat and skin from livers, wash and dry them, then slice. Wash, dry and cube turkey breast. Peel and finely chop shallots. • Heat half butter before frying sliced liver for about 7 minutes over low heat. Keep turning liver while frying, then remove from pan. Sauté chopped shallots in butter until transparent, adding rest of the butter and cubed turkey and continuing to fry over medium heat for 10 minutes. • When breast meat is cool, grind as finely as possible, putting through grinder twice. Finely chop liver and combine with minced meat. Season well with salt, allspice, pepper, marjoram, thyme and sugar, then stir in Armagnac or port. Put in refrigerator to get completely cold. • Beat egg whites with 1 pinch salt until stiff. Whip cream until stiff. • Heat chicken broth, then add gelatin and stir well until completely dissolved. Stir frequently while cooling and leave until it starts to set. • Take parfait out of refrigerator, fold in egg whites and cream together with setting stock. Turn into long earthenware terrine, smooth top, cover with double layer of foil and leave in refrigerator for 24 hours. • Before serving parfait, peel, core and dice apples. Combine in saucepan with sugar, cinnamon and apple juice. Cover pan and simmer gently for 10 minutes, then liquidize or rub through fine sieve. Leave to cool. • Combine elderberry pulp with lemon juice, seasoning to taste with maple syrup, salt and cayenne pepper. • Serve cold parfait with sauces and triangles of hot toast.

Russian Chicken Pie

Requires time and concentration

535 calories per serving
Preparation time: 1 hour
Standing time: 2 hours
Baking time: 30 minutes

Pastry:

1¼ cups flour	
3 tbs. water	
½ tsp. salt	
⅔ cup butter	

Filling:

1¾ lbs. cooked chicken	
¼ cup cutter	
1 cup natural long grain rice	
1 tsp. salt	
2¼ cups mushrooms	
Pinch freshly ground black pepper	
3 hard boiled eggs	
½ cup cream	
Bunch dill	
Bunch parsley	

Glaze:

1 egg yolk	
1 tbs. cream	
Greasing pan: butter	

Sieve flour onto work surface. Make a well in center and put in water and salt, scattering butter in small dabs round edge. Knead all ingredients together as quickly as possible, keeping dough cool. Roll into sausage, wrap in wax paper and put in refrigerator to cool for 2 hours. • To make filling, finely dice cooked chicken. • Melt one half of butter in saucepan, sauté rice briefly, stirring well, then add sufficient water to cover rice. Add ½ tsp. salt, stir once and leave to cook for 20 minutes over low heat until all water is absorbed. • Clean and wipe mushrooms, then slice thinly. Melt remaining butter in sufficiently large frying pan to fry mushrooms; cook over low heat until all juices have evaporated. Season with ½ tsp. salt and pepper. • Peel and chop hard boiled eggs. • Put rice into bowl together with chicken, mushrooms and egg, mixing well while adding cream. • Wash and dry dill and parsley. Cut dill into short feathers, finely chop parsley. Add to filling and season again with salt and pepper to taste. • Preheat oven to 425°F. Grease pan with butter. • Thinly roll out pastry on floured work surface and cut out 2 circles, one exactly the size of the pan, the other slightly bigger. Put larger circle in pan, pressing down well onto base and up sides. Prick base with fork. Spread filling on base and smooth top. Lay pastry lid on top and seal edges together. Prick top to allow steam to escape during baking. • Beat egg yolk with cream and brush over pastry. Bake in middle of oven for 30 minutes until nicely browned. • Serve either hot or cold.

Partridge Pie

Slightly complicated

880 calories per serving
Preparation time: 40 minutes
Baking time: 45 minutes

Pastry:
1¼ cups flour
½ cup butter
1 tsp. salt
1 egg
Filling:
2 roast partridges, each weighing 1¼ lbs.
2 shallots
½ cup button mushrooms
Small bunch basil
10 oz. sausage meat
2 eggs
1 tsp. salt
1 cup sour cream
Pinch hot paprika
Pinch ground ginger
Flour for rolling out

Make short pastry using flour, butter, salt and egg, knead briefly, then put in refrigerator to keep cool until filling is ready. • Take partridge meat off bone, leaving breasts whole and chopping rest. Peel shallots and cut in eighths. Clean and wipe mushrooms. Wash basil and remove thick stalks before finely chopping with partridge, shallots and mushrooms. Combine this with sausage meat, 1 egg, salt, sour cream, paprika and ginger; season very well. • Preheat oven to 400°F. • Divide pastry in two and roll both pieces out on floured surface to form 6 × 12 in. rectangles. • Spoon half of filling onto one pastry rectangle, lay breast pieces on top, cover with rest of filling and finish with second pastry rectangle. Seal edges well together before brushing with beaten egg and cutting slits in lid. • Bake on bottom shelf of oven for 45 minutes.

Chicken Liver Terrine

Easy to prepare but requires certain amount of time

1¼ lbs. chicken liver, as fresh as possible
¼ lb. bacon
2 onions
Sprig fresh thyme
Sprig fresh rosemary
Bunch parsley
2 tbs. dried mushrooms
1 tsp. salt
½ tsp. each, dried thyme and rosemary, ground cloves, cinnamon, mace and ginger
5 tbs. medium sherry
1 lb. 2 oz. sausage meat
1¾ cups sour cream
2 bay leaves
4 thin strips bacon

Clean chicken livers of any bits of fat or skin, rinse quickly under cold tap and pat dry. • Remove fat from bacon piece and finely dice. Peel and chop onions. Rinse herbs in lukewarm water and dry, putting sprigs of thyme and rosemary to one side. Discard thick stalks of parsley and chop leaves. Cover herbs and put aside. • Sauté diced bacon in frying pan, adding onions and frying bacon fat until transparent. Then add chicken livers and sauté for 3 minutes, turning frequently. Next add dried mushrooms, salt, dried herbs and spices; continue to sauté for 1 minute longer, then cool. • Preheat oven to 325°F. Put a good 2 qts. water into pan and bring to a boil. • Coarsely chop liver, then combine with sausage meat, sour cream and chopped parsley. Adjust seasoning if necessary. • Spoon mixture into ovenproof terrine. Lay sprigs of thyme and rosemary on top with bay leaves, then cover with bacon strips. • Seal terrine well with double thickness of foil and place in large pan or roasting pan. Put onto bottom shelf of oven and pour enough boiling water into pan to come to within 1½ in. of top of terrine. • Cook in oven for 45 minutes, making sure that temperature of water stays below 194°F. Check frequently with thermometer and adjust oven temperature accordingly. • Allow terrine to cool in dish. To serve, either cut in slices or use a spoon to scoop out portions. Pickles, cumberland sauce and hot French bread should accompany this dish.

Melt-in-the-Mouth Duck Pie

Requires time for preparation

620 calories per serving
Preparation time: 2½ hours
Baking time: 1 hour

Filling:
2½ qts. water
3 tsp. salt
1 duck weighing 4½ lbs.
Soup vegetables
1 onion
½ bay leaf
2 cloves
½ cup button mushrooms
¼ cup butter
3 tbs. flour
1 egg, separated
2 pinches freshly ground white pepper
½ tsp. dried thyme

Pastry:
2½ cups flour
¾ cups butter
1 egg yolk
½ tsp. salt
½ cup iced water
Butter to grease pan
Egg yolk for glaze

Bring water and 2 tsp. salt to a boil. Wash duck and giblets, then lower duck, heart and gizzard into briskly boiling water. Put liver aside. Simmer duck gently, skimming off scum as it forms during first 30 minutes. • Wash and trim soup vegetables. Peel and halve onion, spiking bay leaf to one half with cloves. After 30 minutes add vegetables to duck and continue to simmer for 1 hour longer. • To make pastry, sieve flour onto work surface with a well in center. Scatter butter in dabs around edge, putting egg yolk, salt and water in well. Work all ingredients lightly together, then roll pastry in foil and leave in refrigerator to chill. • Remove duck from broth, cool slightly, then take meat off bone and finely chop. • Skim fat off cold broth and measure out 1 cup. • Finely chop liver; wipe and chop mushrooms. Heat butter, sauté liver and mushrooms before sprinkling with flour and continuing to sauté until pale brown. Gradually add broth and simmer for 5 minutes, stirring continuously. Take pan off heat, stir in egg yolk and season to taste with salt, pepper and thyme. Stir in minced duck. • Beat egg white until stiff and fold into filling. • Preheat oven to 425°F. Grease pie pan with butter. • Roll out pastry into 2 circles the same size as the pan, plus a long strip to make the side of the pie. Place one circle in base of pan and the long strip round the edge, sealing well. • Spoon filling onto shell, place lid on top and press edges together with a fork. Prick a diamond pattern on top with a skewer so that steam can escape. • Brush with beaten egg yolk. • Bake for 1 hour on bottom shelf of oven and allow to cool in the pan.

Goose in Aspic

Slightly more difficult preparation requiring time

1260 calories per serving
Preparation time: 1 hour
Cooking time: 2 hours
Setting time: 4 hours

1 goose weighing 6½ lbs.	
1 lb. 2 oz. veal bones	
2 onions	
1 tsp. salt	
1 piece lemon peel	
1 bay leaf	
2 cloves	
4 peppercorns	
4 allspice berries	
½ tsp. dried thyme	
Pinch each dried basil and tarragon	
3½ cups water	
2 cups vinegar	
Good quantity soup vegetables	
6 tbs. gelatin	

Large bunch parsley (flat-leaved)

Cut complete leg portions off goose and divide carcass in 4 pieces. Wash all pieces, including neck and gizzard, and put in large saucepan. Wash veal bones as well, and add to pan. Peel and roughly chop onions, adding them with salt, lemon peel, peppercorns, allspice berries, thyme, basil and tarragon to goose. • Bring water to a boil. Pour vinegar over goose, then enough boiling water to cover goose completely. Bring to a boil again, removing any scum as it forms. Cover pan and simmer very gently over low heat for 2 hours. • Trim and wash soup vegetables, add to goose at end of 1 hour. • After 2 full hours, remove pieces of goose and soup vegetables from broth and allow to cool. • Strain broth, then allow to cool before skimming off as much fat

as possible. • Take meat off bone and cut in even cubes. • Cut carrot and celery from soup vegetables into decorative slices using a special knife, if available. • Heat 5 tablespoons broth in saucepan. Dissolve gelatin in hot broth. Add another 4 cups hot broth to gelatin, stirring well, then season generously. • Wash and dry parsley and break leaves off stem. • Rinse out large bowl or mold with cold water and pour in first layer of aspic. Place in refrigerator to set. • Arrange layer of vegetables and parsley leaves on aspic, cover with more aspic and allow to set once more. • Arrange cubed goose and remaining vegetables on second layer, then pour over rest of aspic. • Put in refrigerator for about 4 hours to set completely. • Before serving, loosen aspic around edge of mold with a pointed knife dipped in hot

water, dip mold briefly into hot water and turn out onto plate. • Serve with sauté potatoes and a sweet-and-sour salad of either beetroot or butter beans.

Tip: Keep the goose fat skimmed off broth and use in preparing cabbage or pulse dishes.

Chicken and Fennel Tarts

Economical wholefood recipe

380 calories per serving
Total preparation time: 1½ hours

1 cup wholewheat flour
Pinch salt
Pinch each, freshly ground fennel seed, aniseed and white pepper
½ tsp. baking powder
½ cup butter
2 small eggs
1¾ cup fennel
½ cup chicken broth
14 oz. cooked chicken
1 tbs. each olive oil, lemon juice and mayonnaise
½ tsp. seasoning salt
½ tsp. milk paprika
Pinch cayenne pepper
1 lemon
Butter to grease 6 pans, 3½ in. diameter

Combine flour, salt, fennel seed, aniseed, pepper, baking powder, butter and eggs; knead resulting short pastry lightly. Trim stems of fennel, reserving some of leaves. Wash fennel heads, cut in 8, then cut again in strips ¼ in. thick. Bring chicken broth to a boil and simmer fennel strips, covered, for 15 minutes. Then leave to drain in sieve. • Preheat oven to 350°F. Grease pans with butter. • Roll out pastry and line pans. Bake for 15 minutes, then cool on wire rack. • Dice cooked chicken, combine with fennel, oil, lemon juice, mayonnaise and seasonings. • Cut lemon in thin wedges. • Fill pastry shells with chicken mixture and garnish with wedges of lemon and chopped fennel leaves.

Chicken and Grape Tarts

Popular wholefood recipe

570 calories per serving
Total preparation time: 1 hour

1 cup wholewheat flour
1 tsp. salt
½ tsp. baking powder
2 small eggs
½ cup butter
14 oz. cooked chicken
½ tsp. freshly ground white pepper
2¼ cups green grapes
8 gherkin pickles
1 cup cream cheese
6 tbs. sour cream
2 tbs. tomato paste
¼ tsp. dried basil
18 leaves fresh basil
Butter to grease 6 pans, 3½ in. diameter

Combine flour with ½ tsp. salt and baking powder, make well in center. Break eggs into well and put butter in dabs round edge. Knead all ingredients together quickly. • Finely dice chicken and season with ½ tsp. salt and pepper. Halve and seed grapes. Finely chop pickles. • Using a wire whisk, combine cream cheese, sour cream, tomato paste and dried basil. Add chopped pickles, grapes and diced chicken. • Preheat oven to 350°F. Grease tart pans with butter. • Roll out pastry, line pans and bake in center of oven for 15 minutes. • Leave pastry cases to cool before filling with chicken mixture and garnishing with basil leaves.

Chicken Croissants

A very popular recipe

190 calories per serving
Preparation time: 1 hour
Baking time: 20 minutes

1¼ cups frozen puff pastry
14 oz. boneless chicken breast
1 cup button mushrooms
2 onions
2 tbs. butter
1 tsp. salt
¼ tsp. freshly ground white pepper
1 tsp. dried thyme
2 tbs. cream
1 egg, separated
1 tbs. condensed milk

Remove pastry from wrapping and thaw according to instructions. • Rinse chicken under cold running water, dry well and chop finely. Trim and wipe mushrooms, and finely chop. Peel and dice onions. • Melt butter in large frying pan and fry onion until transparent. Add mushrooms, salt, pepper and thyme, and continue to cook, stirring continuously, until all liquid has evaporated. Take off heat. Stir in cream and leave to cool. • Once cool, mix in egg white and chopped chicken. • Beat egg yolk and condensed milk just enough to combine. • Preheat oven to 400°F. Rinse baking sheet with cold water. • Roll pastry out and cut in 5 squares. Halve each square diagonally, then roll out resulting triangles again to make slightly wider. Put ¹⁄₁₀ of filling along this edge of each triangle, then roll pastry up to form crescent, bending tips around in semi-circle. Brush with egg and milk mixture and put on baking sheet. • Bake for 20 minutes on bottom shelf until evenly browned.

Quail with Truffled Stuffing

Classic, but rather expensive, recipe

700 calories per serving
Total preparation time: 1¼ hours

4 oven-ready quails
1½ tsp. salt
½ tsp. white pepper
2 sprigs fresh basil
7 oz goose liver
1 tbs. butter
Pinch each, salt and freshly ground white pepper
2 tbs. Madeira
2 tsp. truffle (canned)
2 tbs. fresh breadcrumbs
2 tbs. clarified butter
½ head endive
2 small seedless mandarin oranges
2 tbs. orange juice
1 tbs. sunflower oil

Wash and dry quails, then rub inside with 1 tsp. salt and ½ tsp. white pepper. • Wash and dry basil, then finely shred. Wash, dry and cube goose liver. • Melt butter, sauté liver, season with pinch each of salt and pepper. Add 1 tbs. Madeira and stew uncovered for 5 minutes. Finely chop truffle before combining with basil, breadcrumbs and liver. • Preheat oven to 400°F. • Stuff quails with mixture, sew up openings and truss. • Heat clarified butter in roasting pan, brown quails thoroughly, then put in bottom of oven for 20 minutes to roast. • Pick over, wash and shred endive. Peel mandarin oranges and cut in segments. Combine orange juice with ½ tsp. salt, remaining Madeira and oil. Pour over mandarin segments and endive and toss. • Remove quail from oven, cool, then remove trussing string and serve arranged on endive salad.

Chicken with Broccoli

Well-known recipe

670 calories per serving
Preparation time: 1 hour
Cooking time: 30 minutes

1 chicken weighing 2¾ lbs.	
1 onion	
1 carrot	
1 stick celery	
2 tbs. coconut fat	
3 tbs. sherry vinegar	
1 cup water	
1 sprig thyme	
1½ tsp. salt	
8 small flat onions	
3½ cups broccoli	
1 tsp. sugar	
1 tbs. butter	
5 tbs. orange juice	
½ tsp. freshly ground white pepper	
¼ cup corn oil	

Wash chicken, cut in 8 pieces and dry well. • Peel onions and cut in eighths. Scrape and wash carrot, clean celery, then chop both. • Brown chicken pieces in coconut fat, frying vegetables at same time. Add vinegar, water, thyme and 1 tsp. salt, then cover and simmer for 30 minutes. • Peel onions. Clean and wash broccoli before dividing in florets. • Take chicken pieces out of cooking liquid. Strain broth, then boil onions in it for 10 minutes. Remove from broth. Boil broccoli for 10 minutes in 2 cups water, then drain and cool. • Allow sugar to caramelize to a light brown in butter, add onions and glaze. • Toss broccoli in dressing made from orange juice, ½ tsp. salt, pepper and oil. Serve chicken arranged on dish with broccoli and glazed onions.

Goose and Brussels Sprouts Vinaigrette

Easy to prepare

640 calories per serving
Preparation time: 45 minutes
Cooking time: 40 minutes

4 goose drumsticks, each weighing ¾ lbs.	
1 onion	
1 carrot	
3 tbs. coconut	
2 tsp. salt	
3 cups hot chicken broth	
6 tbs. white wine vinegar	
6 tbs. medium sherry	
3½ cups Brussels sprouts	
1 large tart apple	
2 shallots	
2 tsp. lemon juice	
2 tbs. sunflower oil	
Good pinch sugar	
1 tbs. chopped parsley	

Wash goose. Peel onion and cut in eighths. Scrape, wash, dry and chop carrot. • heat coconut fat in a large pan. Brown drumsticks over high heat, then sprinkle with 1 tsp. salt before adding vegetables and continue to fry. Pour in broth, vinegar and sherry, bring to a boil again and simmer goose for 40 minutes. Remove drumsticks from broth and cool. Strain broth and boil to reduce to 1 cup. • Clean and wash Brussels sprouts, put in saucepan with 1 tsp. salt and water to cover. Boil for 20 minutes, then strain. • Peel, core and quarter apple, then thinly slice quarters. Combine lemon juice with oil, sugar, parsley, reduced broth, Brussels sprouts and apple slices, mixing thoroughly. Arrange on serving dish with goose drumsticks.

Larded Breast of Turkey

Slightly more difficult

400 calories per serving
Preparation time: 40 minutes
Cooking time: 40 minutes

2¼ lb. turkey breast (in one piece)	
2 oz. lean bacon	
½ tsp. salt	
½ tsp. freshly ground white pepper	
2 tsp. milk paprika	
¼ cup light white wine	
2 small heads radicchio	
Pinch each, salt and freshly ground white pepper	
1 cup fresh pineapple	
2 tsp. lemon juice	
2 tbs. white wine	
2 tsp. honey	

Cut bacon in strips ¼ in. wide and put in freezer to become firm. • Wash and dry turkey breast. • Preheat oven to 400°F. Take cold rack out of oven. • Lard turkey breast evenly with bacon, using a larding needle. Rub salt, pepper and paprika into meat and lay on piece of aluminum foil. Sprinkle over white wine and seal foil well all round, piercing top several times with a needle. Place on cold rack, slide into bottom shelf of oven and bake for 40 minutes. • Rinse radicchio well without splitting up, arrange on serving dish and sprinkle with pinch each salt and pepper. Peel pineapple and cut into small cubes, removing hard core. Arrange cubes on radicchio and sprinkle with lemon juice. Heat 2 tbs. white wine, dissolve honey in it and sprinkle mixture over radicchio salad. • Allow turkey to cool, then carve in thin slices and ar-range on dish with salad. Sprinkle cold cooking juices over turkey slices.

Breast of Duck with Chicory Salad

330 calories per serving
Total preparation time: 20 minutes

2 duck breasts, boned but with skin, each weighing 10 oz.	
2 tbs. clarified butter	
1 tsp. salt	
½ tsp. freshly ground white pepper	
3 heads chicory	
2 tomatoes	
1 cup zucchini	
1 onion	
1 tbs. lemon juice	
1 tbs. maple syrup	
2 tbs. walnut oil	
1 tbs. chopped chives	

Wash and dry duck breasts, then sauté for 15 minutes in clarified butter. Sprinkle with pepper and ½ tsp. salt and leave to cool. • Trim chicory, wash in lukewarm water, dry and slice in rings. • Cut a shallow cross in skin of tomatoes, plunge into boiling water, skin and finely dice. Peel and dice zucchini. Peel onion and finely chop. • Combine all salad ingredients with remaining salt, lemon juice, maple syrup and oil, sprinkling chives over top. • Carve duck in thin slices and arrange with salad on serving platter.

Barded Breast of Pheasant

Rather more expensive

790 calories per serving
Total preparation time: 1 hour

2 young pheasants, each weighing 2¼ lbs.
1 tsp. salt
2 good pinches white pepper
2 fresh sprigs sage or 1 tsp. dried sage
2 tbs. clarified butter
2 oz. lean bacon cut very thin
1¼ cups sweet chestnuts
1 tbs. butter
2 tsp. sugar

Wash and dry pheasants, then rub well inside with salt and pepper. Rinse and dry fresh sage, or crush dried variety. Rub half the sage inside pheasants. • Preheat oven to 425°F. •

Heat clarified butter and brown pheasants over heat for 5 minutes. Place them in roasting pan, sprinkle with remaining fat from frying pan, then cover breasts with bacon slices and roast on bottom shelf of oven for 30 minutes. • Cut a cross just through skins of chestnuts and cook them in rapidly boiling water for 20 minutes. • Remove pheasants from oven and allow to cool. • Rinse chestnuts under cold water and then peel. • Caramelize sugar in butter until light brown, add chestnuts and glaze, stirring until they are evenly coated with syrup. Put aside to cool. • Cut breast portions from pheasants, putting aside remainder of birds to be used in other dishes. Carve breast meat with bacon layer in slices ½ in. thick, arrange on serving dish with glazed chestnuts and sprinkle with remaining sage.

Breast of Chicken with Kiwi Fruit

Quick and easy to prepare

310 calories per serving
Total preparation time: 45 minutes

1¾ lbs. chicken breasts, on bone and with skin
4 cups chicken broth
1 stalk celery
1 leek
4 kiwi fruits
1 orange
1 lemon
1 tbs. butter
1 tbs. sugar
Pinch salt
Pinch cayenne pepper

Wash chicken breasts. Bring chicken broth to a boil. Simmer chicken in broth for 10 minutes, removing any scum that

forms. • Trim and wash celery and leek, then chop and add to broth. Poach chicken and vegetables very gently for 10 minutes longer. • Peel kiwi fruit and cut in ¼ in. thick slices. Arrange slices in fan-shaped pattern on serving dish. • Wash orange in hot water, then dry and peel one half very thinly. Finely shred this peel and scatter over kiwi fruit. • Squeeze orange and lemon. • Melt butter and caramelize sugar in it, then add citrus juice very gradually, stirring well. Reduce sauce to 2 tbs. and season with salt and cayenne pepper. • Take chicken off bone, removing any skin, and cut in slices. Arrange on serving dish with kiwi fruit and pour orange sauce over meat.

Chicken with Anchovy Mayonnaise

Requires a certain amount of time for preparation

550 calories per serving
Preparation time: 30 minutes
Cooking time: 1½ hours
Cooling time: 2 hours

1 roasting chicken weighing 2¾ lbs.
1 bunch parsley
3 sprigs fresh basil
Soup vegetables
1 onion
1 bay leaf
1 clove
4 oz. canned tuna
4 anchovies
1 tbs. capers
1 gherkin pickle
¼ cup mayonnaise (reduced fat)
1 tsp. lemon juice
Pinch each salt and freshly ground white pepper

Wash chicken both inside and out, then place in large saucepan. Wash sprigs of basil and parsley stalks and add to chicken, together with prepared soup vegetables. Peel and halve onion, spike bay leaf on one half with clove and add both pieces to chicken. Pour on sufficient boiling water to cover chicken well. • Boil chicken for 30 minutes, removing any scum as it forms, then reduce heat and poach gently for 1 hour longer. • Drain tuna and finely chop with anchovies, capers and gherkin pickle. Stir this mixture into mayonnaise, seasoning to taste with lemon juice, salt and pepper. Finely chop parsley and add to mayonnaise. • Cool chicken in broth before cutting in serving portions and arranging on platter. • Serve anchovy mayonnaise separately.

Chicken in Tarragon Sauce

Easy to make

570 calories per serving
Preparation time: 20 minutes
Cooking time: 40 minutes
Chilling time: 1 hour

1 roasting chicken weighing 2¾ lbs.
2 cloves garlic
¼ cup olive oil
2 bay leaves
Juice of 1 lemon
Scant 1 cup dry white wine
¼ cup tarragon vinegar
1 tsp. salt
Pinch white pepper
1 tbs. freshly chopped tarragon
½ lemon
12 black olives

Peel garlic and chop finely. Wash chicken, cut in 8 pieces and dry. • Heat oil, brown chicken pieces together with garlic and bay leaves, then sprinkle with lemon juice. Add wine, vinegar, salt and pepper to pan, cover and simmer on low heat for 40 minutes, turning chicken pieces several times. • Remove chicken from cooking liquid, turn up heat and reduce liquid rapidly. • Arrange chicken pieces on serving platter, spoon over chilled, reduced cooking liquid and sprinkle with chopped tarragon. Wash and dry lemon, cut in 8 wedges and use with olives as garnish.

Marinated Chicken Legs

Easy to prepare

450 calories per serving
Preparation time: 15 minutes
Marinating time: 3 hours
Cooking time: 45 minutes

8 chicken legs, each weighing 6 oz.
2 cloves garlic
1 small fresh red chili
1 cup dry white wine
1 tbs. Dijon mustard
1 tsp. mixed herbs
Pinch freshly ground black pepper
1 tsp. salt
6 tbs. olive oil

Peel garlic and chop finely. Remove stem and seeds from chili, wash and dry it, then cut in fine rings. Combine with garlic, wine, mustard, herbs and pepper to make the marinade. • Wash and dry chicken legs, rub well with salt and place in a flat ovenproof dish. Pour marinade over chicken, cover dish and put in refrigerator to marinate for 3 hours. Turn legs several times during marinating. • Preheat oven to 400°F. • Take chicken legs out of dish, pouring marinade into another container. Brush chicken with oil and return to original dish. Place in center of oven and roast for 45 minutes, basting with marinade several times. • After 35 minutes switch oven to 475°F, move chicken up to top shelf and cook there for last 10 minutes so that the chicken legs turn a crisp golden brown. • Allow chicken to cool and serve coated with remaining marinade.

Tip: If more chicken legs are required, they can be cooked in a big roasting pan.

Turkey Breast with Spinach Filling

Rather more expensive and time-consuming

600 calories per serving
Preparation time: 1 hour
Cooking time: 1½ hours
Standing time: 6 hours

1 turkey breast weighing 3¼ lbs., boned and skinned
1¾ cup young spinach
2 medium onions
2 cloves garlic
1 bread roll
½ cup Parmesan cheese
¼ cup cream cheese
2 tbs. olive oil
1 egg
2 tbs. fresh breadcrumbs
2 tbs. slivered almonds
½ tsp. salt
½ tsp. dried oregano
Pinch freshly ground black pepper
Pinch freshly grated nutmeg
½ tsp. dried thyme
¼ cup coconut oil
½ cup boiling water
1 cup button mushrooms
2 shallots
1 bunch parsley
1 tbs. butter
Pinch each salt and freshly ground white pepper
2 cups cream
2 cups sour cream

Pick over spinach and wash it, then place, with no extra water, in saucepan and cook carefully until tender. Drain in sieve and chop. • Peel onion and garlic, then chop both finely. • Soak bread roll in cold water. • Grate Parmesan and dice cream cheese. • Heat oil in frying pan and sauté onion and garlic gently for 5 minutes without browning. Add spinach and continue to heat, stirring well, until all liquid has evaporated. Transfer to a bowl. • Squeeze water out of bread roll and crumble. Combine with cheese, egg, breadcrumbs, slivered almonds, salt, oregano, pepper and nutmeg, and stir into spinach mixture. Season this filling well. • Preheat oven to 400°F. • Sew up cuts in turkey breast where bones were removed. Cut a deep slit in breast to form a pocket. Fill with spinach mixture and sew up. • Rub well with salt, pepper and thyme and put in roasting pan. Heat coconut fat until very hot and pour over turkey. Put in bottom of oven and roast for 1½ hours, pouring hot water frequently into pan and basting turkey with cooking juices. • To make the sauce, trim, wipe and slice mushrooms thinly. Peel and chop shallots. Wash, dry and chop parsley. • Heat butter in frying-pan, sauté mushrooms for 3 minutes over high heat, then add shallots and parsley and sauté together. Season with salt and pepper and take off heat. Stir in cream and sour cream, then cover and chill. • When turkey is cool, wrap in foil and put in refrigerator for 6 hours. • Carve turkey in slices and serve with the cold sauce.

Turkey Liver Pate on Wholewheat Crackers

Economical, wholefood recipe

81 calories per serving
Preparation time: 45 minutes
Baking time: 10 minutes

1¾ cups wholewheat flour
Pinch each salt, curry powder, white pepper and mild paprika
½ tsp. baking powder
1 egg
½ cup butter
1 tbs. sesame seeds
1 onion
1 tbs. butter
7 oz. turkey liver
Pinch black pepper
3 tbs. cream
½ tsp. each freshly chopped thyme and marjoram
2 tsp. freshly chopped parsley
Pinch sea salt
Butter for greasing baking sheet

Combine flour with salt, curry powder, pepper, paprika and baking powder, then make a well in center and break egg into it. Put butter in dabs around edge and gradually knead all ingredients together. Roll dough into a sausage 6 in. long and 2 in. thick, before coating in sesame seeds and pressing in well. • Peel and finely chop onion, then sauté in butter until light brown. Remove all fat and membrane from liver, wash and dry and cut in 1 in. pieces. Add to onions in frying-pan and continue to fry, covered, for 5 minutes, stirring well. Then cool, season with pepper and liquidize to a smooth cream together with pan juices, cream, thyme and marjoram. Stir in chopped parsley and season to taste with salt. • Preheat oven to 400°F. Grease a baking sheet with butter. • Cut dough sausage into ¼ in. thick slices and bake for 10 minutes in oven. • Cool crackers on wire stand before spreading with a thick layer of pate and garnishing according to taste.

Mango and Turkey Salad

Easy-to-prepare wholefood recipe

430 calories per serving
Total preparation time: 50 minutes

| 3 boneless turkey breasts, each weighing 6 oz. |
| 1 cup brown long grain rice |
| 1 tsp. cardamon seeds |
| ½ tsp. each salt and curry powder |
| 3 cups water |
| Juice of ½ lemon |
| Generous pinch freshly ground white pepper |
| 1 ripe mango weighing 10 oz. |
| 2 tbs. sour cream |
| 2 tbs. sesame oil |
| 2 tbs. lemon juice |
| ¼ cup chicken broth with all fat removed |
| 2 tbs. dill |
| ¼ cup sesame seeds |

Put rice in saucepan with cardamon, ¼ tsp. salt, ¼ tsp. curry powder and water, put lid on and cook very gently over low heat for 35 minutes. • Wash and dry turkey, then sprinkle with lemon juice and pepper. Lay turkey on top of rice during last 10 minutes of cooking time, turning over after 5 minutes. • Drain rice in a sieve. Cut turkey in strips. • Wash and dry mango, then cut in slices lengthwise around pit. Peel resulting pieces, before cutting some in long thin slices and chopping the rest. • Combine rice with turkey strips, chopped mango, sour cream, sesame oil, lemon juice, chicken stock, remaining salt and curry powder and dill. Taste and adjust seasoning. • Toast sesame seeds in frying pan without fat, stirring well until browned. Sprinkle over rice salad arranged on serving plate and garnished with dill and sliced mango.

Indian Rice Salad

Easy-to-prepare wholefood recipe

310 calories per serving
Total preparation time: 45 minutes

| 7 oz. cooked chicken |
| 1 cup brown long grain rice |
| ½ chicken bouillon cube |
| 2 bananas |
| 1 tsp. lemon juice |
| 1¼ cups full cream yogurt |
| 1 tbs. sour cream |
| 1 tbs. sesame oil |
| 2 tbs. white wine vinegar |
| ½ cup chicken broth with all fat removed |
| 1 onion |
| 1 small red chili |
| ¾ cup fresh pineapple, peeled |
| 1-2 tsp. freshly grated green ginger |
| 1 tsp. curry powder |
| 1 sprig lemon balm |

Cook rice with water and bouillon cube in covered pan for 35 minutes over low heat until done. • Cut chicken in thin strips. Peel bananas, slicing one and sprinkling with lemon juice. Mash second banana and combine with yogurt, sour cream, oil, vinegar and chicken broth, stirring to a smooth sauce. • Peel and finely chop onion. Cut chili in half, remove seeds and chop finely. Cut pineapple into small cubes. • Mix rice with chicken, pineapple cubes, sliced banana, chopped onion and chili, fold in yogurt sauce and season with ginger, curry powder

and perhaps a little salt to taste. • Chop half lemon balm and stir into salad, using remaining leaves as garnish.

Quail Salad

Suitable as a first course

310 calories per serving
Total preparation time: 1 hour

| 4 quails, each weighing 6 oz. |
| 1 tsp. salt |
| 4 black peppercorns |
| 1 stick celery |
| 2 shallots |
| 1 small head radicchio |
| ¼ head endive |
| ¼ lb. lamb's lettuce |
| 1 small orange |
| 1 tbs. freshly squeezed orange juice |
| 1 tbs. sherry vinegar |
| Good pinch each salt and black pepper |
| 2 tbs. olive oil |
| 2 tbs. butter |

Wash quail, put in saucepan with salt and peppercorns, cover with boiling water and bring back to a boil. Skim off any scum as it forms. • Trim, wash and finely chop celery. Peel and quarter shallots, add with celery to saucepan and poach for 30 minutes very gently, making sure water only just moves. • Wash, pick over and drain radicchio, endive and lamb's lettuce. • Tear radicchio in bite-sized pieces, shred endive and mix all three kinds together. • Peel orange, cut in rounds, dividing each round in 4, then sprinkle over salad. Combine orange juice with vinegar, salt, pepper and oil for dressing. • Remove skin from quails, cut off breast meat in one piece and set aside. Chop rest of meat. • Melt butter and sauté quail breasts for 1 minute on each side, tossing rest of meat briefly in hot butter. • Pour dressing over salad and arrange warm quail meat on top.

Chicken and Maize Salad

Easily prepared wholefood recipe

260 calories per serving
Preparation time: 40 minutes
Cooking time: 1 hour

| 14 oz. cooked chicken |
| 1 cup coarsely ground maize (polenta) |
| 3 cups water |
| ½ vegetable bouillon cube |
| 1 green pepper |
| 1 red pepper |
| 2 medium tomatoes |
| 2 tbs. olive oil |
| 1-2 tbs. cider vinegar |
| 1 tsp. freshly chopped rosemary |
| 1 tsp. freshly chopped thyme |
| ½ tsp. milk paprika |
| Pinch freshly ground black pepper |
| 2 tbs. chopped chives |

Bring ground maize to a boil with water and bouillon cube, cover saucepan tightly, switch off hotplate and leave there for just under an hour to swell. • Cut peppers in quarters lengthwise, removing stem and seeds, then blanch for 5 minutes in boiling salted water. Drain and cut in thin strips. • Skin and quarter tomatoes. • Shred chicken. • When maize is cooked, combine it with oil, vinegar, herbs, paprika, pepper, shredded green and red pepper and chicken. Mix well. Arrange tomato on top and garnish with chopped chives.

Chicken and Asparagus Salad

Makes an excellent first course

500 calories per serving
Preparation time: 40 minutes
Cooking time: 1¾ hours

1 chicken weighing 2¼ lbs.	
1½ tsp. salt	
½ onion	
¼ bay leaf	
1 clove	
⅔ cup leeks	
1 medium carrot	
1 small piece celery	
4½ cups asparagus	
2 tbs. cider vinegar	
Pinch white pepper	
Pinch sugar	
¼ cup corn oil	
2 tbs. chopped chives	

Wash chicken and giblets, sprinkle with 1 tsp. salt, cover with water and bring to a boil. Skim off any scum that forms during first 15 minutes. Then turn heat down and poach chicken very gently for 1½ hours. • Peel onion, spike bay leaf onto it with clove and add to chicken. • Trim, wash and slice leek. Scrape and wash carrot, then cut into sticks. Peel, wash and halve celery. • After chicken has cooked for 30 minutes, add prepared vegetables to pan and continue to cook uncovered for remaining time. • Wash asparagus and peel stems where necessary. • At end of cooking time, remove chicken from pan, straining broth and returning it to pan. Bring back to a boil. Cut asparagus in 2 in. lengths and simmer stem pieces in broth for 15 minutes, adding asparagus tips after 8 minutes. • Take chicken meat off bone and cut in even pieces. • Tip asparagus into sieve, reserving broth to use elsewhere. Allow chicken and asparagus to cool. • Mix cider vinegar with ½ tsp. salt, pepper, sugar and oil, then stir this dressing into chicken and asparagus. Sprinkle with chives before serving.

Duck and Chanterelle Salad

Excellent as a starter

230 calories per serving
Total preparation time: 45 minutes

1 cup chanterelles	
1 boned duck breast, weighing 10 oz.	
Pinch black pepper	
½ tsp. dried marjoram	
¼ cup walnut oil	
1 oz. lean bacon	
1 small head oak-leaf lettuce	
2 shallots	
¼ cup white wine vinegar	
½ tsp. salt	

Clean, rinse and drain chanterelles. • Wash and dry duck breast, rub well with pepper and marjoram, sauté in 1 tablespoon oil for 5 minutes on each side then remove from frying pan. • Finely dice bacon and sauté in same pan until evenly brown. Add chanterelles and sauté for 2 minutes with bacon. • Pick over, wash and drain oak-leaf lettuce. Peel shallots, chop finely and combine with vinegar, salt and remaining oil, then toss salad in this dressing. • Carve duck in thin slices and arrange with chanterelles on salad to serve.

Duck Liver and Red Cabbage Salad

Easy to prepare

400 calories per serving
Total preparation time: 50 minutes

14 oz. duck liver	
Pinch each cinnamon, ground cloves, crushed coriander and dried thyme	
2¼ cups red cabbage	
1½ tsp. salt	
5 tbs. red wine vinegar	
¼ cup sunflower oil	
1 head lettuce	
8 strips bacon cut very thin (2 oz.)	
Pinch white pepper	
6 tbs. medium sherry	
2 tbs. cream	
1 tsp. lemon juice	
Pinch each salt and pepper	
4 pear halves, canned	
¼ cup red currant jelly	

Remove any fat or membrane from livers, rinse under cold water, pat dry, then cut in 1 in. cubes. Combine with cinnamon, ground cloves, coriander and thyme. • Quarter red cabbage and shred as finely as possible, before pounding for 5 minutes with a rolling pin. • Combine 1 tsp. salt, vinegar and oil, then toss cabbage in dressing. • Arrange leaves from lettuce heart on serving dish. • Brown strips of bacon in frying pan until crisp, then remove from pan. Sauté liver in bacon fat for 5 minutes, season with salt and pepper, add 5 tbs. sherry and keep warm. • Mix together cream with lemon juice, ½ tsp. salt, pepper and remaining sherry; sprinkle this dressing over lettuce. Arrange red cabbage over lettuce, with liver and pan juices on top. Crumble bacon over salad. Fill hollow in pear halves with red currant jelly and arrange on salad platter.

Turkey and Barley Salad

Easily prepared wholefood recipe

500 calories per serving
Soaking time: 12 hours
Preparation time: 30 minutes
Cooking time: 50 minutes

1¼ cups pot barley
4 cups water
1 turkey drumstick weighing 1¾ lbs.
2 pinches freshly ground black pepper
Soup vegetables
½ cup pitted prunes
1 leek, white part only (2 oz.)
1 vegetable bouillon cube
2 tbs. sunflower oil
2 tbs. red wine vinegar
2 tbs. sour cream
½ tsp. salt

Put barley and water in container, cover and soak for 12 hours. • Transfer barley and water to saucepan large enough to take turkey drumstick as well. Wash and dry drumstick, rub well with a pinch of pepper and place on barley in pan. Cover pan and simmer gently for 50 minutes until done, turning drumstick over after 30 minutes. • Trim, wash and chop soup vegetables, then add to turkey for final 15 minutes cooking time, with more water if required. Drain barley in sieve. Take meat off bone and cut in 1¼ in. pieces, sprinkling with remaining pepper. • Rinse prunes in warm water, then dry and quarter them. Wash and dry leek, then cut in very thin rings. • Bring 1 cup water to a boil and dissolve bouillon cube in it. • Combine barley with prunes, leek, turkey, bouillon, oil, vinegar, sour cream and salt, tasting and adding a little more red wine vinegar and salt if desired.

Turkey Breast and Potato Salad

Economical wholefood recipe

500 calories per serving
Preparation time: 40 minutes
Cooking time: 30 minutes

3 cups salad potatoes
Scant 1 cup chicken broth
2 red onions
2 ripe avocados
2 pinches freshly ground black pepper
3-4 tbs. white wine vinegar
2 tbs. sunflower oil
10 oz. smoked turkey breast
½-1 tsp. seasoning salt
2 tbs. fresh dill

Scrub potatoes well under running cold water, put in saucepan, cover with water and bring to a boil. Put lid on pan and cook for 30 minutes until done. • Bring chicken broth to a boil. • Peel onions, cut in quarters lengthwise, then in very thin slices across the quarters. • Cut avocados in half lengthwise, remove pit and peel. Then halve again lengthwise and slice resulting quarters. • Drain cooked potatoes, rinse with cold water, then peel and dice. Add hot broth and pepper to diced potatoes, then sliced onion and avocado with vinegar and oil. • Dice turkey breast and stir into potato salad, seasoning with seasoning salt. • Sprinkle with chopped dill before serving.

Duck Salad

Easy-to-prepare wholefood recipe

430 calories per serving
Total preparation time: 50 minutes

½ cup groats (i.e. hulled and crushed oat kernels)
3 cups chicken broth
1¾ cups Savoy cabbage
4 cups water
1 tsp. salt
1 red onion
14 oz. cooked duck, off bone
1 tbs. sunflower oil
2 tbs. red wine vinegar
1 tsp. Worcestershire sauce
Pinch freshly ground black pepper

Stir groats into chicken broth, bring to a boil, and boil for 5 minutes, then turn heat down as far as possible and leave pan, covered, for 40 minutes to finish cooking. • Wash cabbage, cut away thick stem and any bad bits before finely shredding leaves. Blanch shredded cabbage for 5 minutes in boiling salted water and drain in sieve. • Peel onions, quarter lengthwise and slice thinly across quarters. Cut duck in thin strips. • Drain cooked oats in sieve. • Combine suntil warm oats with cabbage, oil, vinegar, Worcestershire sauce and pepper, adding a little broth from oats if necessary. • Arrange onion and duck on top of salad shortly before serving.

Turkey Salad with Celery

Easy to prepare and good as hors d'oeuvres

210 calories per serving
Total preparation time: 30 minutes

1¼ cups celery	
2 yellow peppers	
14 oz. smoked turkey breast	
1 small onion	
¼ cup mayonnaise (low fat)	
1 low fat yogurt (6 oz.)	
2 tsp. hot mustard	
1 tsp. maple syrup	
½ tsp. salt	
Pinch freshly ground white pepper	

Separate celery into stalks, cut off green tops, rinse in lukewarm water, dry and put aside. Wash and dry stalks, re-moving any coarse strings. Slice in ½ in. pieces. • Halve peppers, remove stem and seeds, wash and dry, then cut in strips. Carve turkey in slices ½ in. thick, then cut slices in ½ in. strips. • Peel and grate onion before combin-ing with mayonnaise, yogurt, mustard, maple syrup, salt and pepper. • Toss all salad ingre-dients lightly in dressing, then cover and allow to stand at room temperature for about 10 min-utes before serving. • Serve with crackers and garnish with green celery tops.

Chicken and Orange Salad

Quick and easy to prepare

600 calories per serving
Total preparation time: 30 minutes

1 grilled or roast chicken weighing 2¾ lbs.	
2 medium oranges	
2 slices fresh pineapple	
1 cup cooked long grain rice	
2 tbs. pineapple juice	
1 tbs. fresh orange juice	
½ tsp. salt	
2 egg yolks	
1 tsp. mild mustard	
1 pinch hot paprika	
¼ cup oil	
5 mint leaves	

Remove skin from chicken and take meat off bone, cut-ting it in even pieces. • Peel or-anges carefully, removing all white strings, then separate in segments. Quarter segments and remove any pits. • Cut skin off pineapple and cut in wedges. • Combine chicken pieces with rice and prepared orange and pineapple. • Mix pineapple juice, orange juice and salt. Whisk egg yolks with mustard and paprika, adding oil drop by drop and whisking continuously until a thick mayonnaise forms. Stir fruit juice into this mayonnaise, then fold into salad. • Rinse mint leaves in lukewarm water, pat dry, then shred and sprinkle over salad.

Tip: If you have more time avail-able, poach a chicken yourself and use instead of the ready-cooked one, serving the broth as a soup course before the salad.

Turkey Cocktail in Yogurt Sauce

Classic recipe, though rather more expensive

500 calories per serving
Total preparation time: 1½ hours

4 cups water
1 tsp. salt
1 turkey drumstick weighing 2¼ lbs.
2 bananas
2 apples (Macintosh)
Juice of ½ lemon
1 small pineapple
1¾ cups black grapes
1¾ cups whipping cream
2½ cups full cream yogurt
Pinch each salt and freshly ground white pepper
1 liqueur glass brandy (½ oz.)
6 sprigs mint

Bring water and salt to a boil, put in washed turkey drumstick, cover and simmer for 1 hour. • Peel bananas, halve lengthwise and slice. Quarter, peel, core and dice apples, then mix with sliced banana and sprinkle with lemon juice. • Slice pineapple, halve each slice, cut away skin and hard core, then cut in small cubes. Wash and dry grapes, then halve and remove pit. • When drumstick is cool enough to handle, take meat off bone, dice and cool. • Whip cream until stiff, then combine with yogurt, salt, pepper and brandy, Pour this sauce over fruit and turkey and mix well. • Garnish with mint sprigs.

Chicken and Fruit Salad

Easy to prepare, though rather more expensive

290 calories per serving
Total preparation time: 40 minutes

1¼ lbs. boneless chicken breasts
2 tbs. clarified butter
1 tsp. salt
½ tsp. white pepper
2¼ cups strawberries
¾ cup bean sprouts
2 tsp. chopped preserved ginger
1 tbs. ginger syrup
1 tbs. basil vinegar
1 tbs. soy sauce
Pinch each salt and cayenne pepper
2 tbs. olive oil

Wash chicken thoroughly, then dry and remove skin if necessary. Cut in strips ½ in. thick. • Heat clarified butter and sauté chicken strips for 8 minutes, turning frequently, then season with salt and pepper before removing from pan and draining on paper towel. Allow to cool. • Rinse strawberries several times in warm water, drain well and hull, halving any big berries. Wash and pick over bean sprouts, then combine with strawberries, cooled chicken and diced ginger in a bowl. • Mix ginger syrup with vinegar, soy sauce, salt and cayenne pepper, adding oil and tossing salad gently in resulting dressing. • Cover salad and leave for 10 minutes at room temperature for flavor to fully develop.

Index